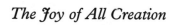

The Joy of All Creation

The Joy of All Creation

An Anglican Meditation on the Place of Mary

A.M. ALLCHIN

Foreword by
Edward Yarnold s.j.

New City
London Dublin Edinburgh

First published in 1984 by
Darton, Longman and Todd Ltd
Second edition substantially revised
and with new material
published in 1993 by New City
57 Twyford Avenue, London W5 9PZ

British Library Cataloguing in Publication Data:

A catalogue reference for this book
can be obtained from the British Library

ISBN 0 904287 48 3

Set in Linotype Sabon and Monotype Plantin by
Phoenix Typesetting, Ilkley, West Yorkshire

Printed and bound by
The Cromwell Press, Broughton Gifford, Wiltshire

For Anna-Marie Aagaard,
friend and theologian

Contents

Acknowledgements

Excerpts from 'Burnt Norton' and 'The Dry Salvages' in *Four Quartets* by T.S. Eliot are reprinted by permission of Faber and Faber Ltd and Harcourt Brace Jovanovich Inc; copyright 1943 by T.S. Eliot; renewed 1971 by Esme Valerie Eliot. Excerpts from *Collected Poems* by Edwin Muir are reprinted by permission of Faber and Faber Ltd and Oxford University Press Inc, New York; copyright 1960 by Willa Muir. The devotion by Thomas Traherne printed on pp. 117-19 is reproduced by courtesy of the Curators of the Bodleian Library, Oxford (MS. Eng. th. e 51). Excerpts from *The Paperbark Tree: Selected Prose* by Les Murray are reprinted by permission of Carcanet; copyright 1992 by Les Murray. Excerpts from *Lancelot Andrewes the Preacher* by Nicholas Lossky are reprinted by permission of Oxford University Press; copyright 1991 by Nicholas Lossky.

Foreword

Having been associated with Donald Allchin over the past thirty years in a number of ecumenical endeavours, often in connection with the Ecumenical Society of the Blessed Virgin Mary, it has given me great pleasure to be asked to contribute this foreword to his Anglican vision of Mary as the Joy of Creation.

'Modern Anglican theology', wrote a former Archbishop of Canterbury,[1] 'owes many of its characteristics to the central place held within it by the Incarnation.'[1] Canon Allchin sees in the Anglican writers he studies the truths of the Incarnation and the Church coming together in the person of Mary. In all three areas of doctrine there is exemplified the sacramental principle that God comes to his people through the medium of created things.

It has been one of the insights of recent ecumenical theology that the unity of Christians to which Christ calls us is not a blend in which all differentiation is lost, but a skein in which the different traditions retain their distinct and complementary identity. Pope Paul VI spoke of 'the living beauty of the bride of Christ, the Church, wrapped in her many-coloured garment, clothed, we mean, in a legitimate pluralism of traditional expressions'.[2] As Canon Allchin shows, the Anglican thread that is woven into this particoloured Christian understanding of our Lady has two special qualities: it prefers poetic imagery to abstract speculation, and it expresses joy.

For Lancelot Andrewes in the seventeenth century, Mary is the Land of Promise, the good earth which brings forth the Saviour. For the poet Henry Vaughan she is 'the true love's knot', by whom 'God is made our ally'; 'the glad world's blessed maid,/ Whose beauty brought life to thy house'. Jeremy Taylor sees the 'two glories' of mother and maid meeting in her like the sun and the moon; in the fullness of her joy 'she was carried like a full vessel', with 'a quietness symbolical to the holy guest of her spotless womb'. In her 'quiet and silent piety' the Holy Ghost descended on her 'like rain into a fleece of wool'. Her reticence about the Annunciation, even to Joseph, is 'like rain falling in uninhabited valleys, where no eye observes the showers; yet the valleys laugh and sing to God in their refreshment without a witness'. Taylor muses on the 'collision of joys' at the Visitation, when 'two mothers of two great princes meet'. For Mark Frank 'the glorious Virgin's lap' is 'the shrine and altar. . . where the Saviour of the world is laid to be adored and worshipped'. Thomas Traherne's litany of praise of God for the Blessed Virgin speaks of her as 'nearest unto Thee, in the Throne of God. . . Tabernacle of the most glorious Trinity. . . The most Illustrious Light in the Church, Wearing over all her Beauties the veil of Humility'. Thoman Ken saw heavenly glory which crowns the divine Infant dilating to surround his mother.

In the nineteenth century, Anglican writing on Mary is less exuberant, but no less joyous. Addressing the 'Virgin-born', Bishop Reginald Heber exclaims, 'Blessed was the parent's eye/ That watched thy slumbering infancy'. For John Keble the 'Sacramental Touch of the Church' is 'the Touch of Christ', in which Mary is 'especially instrumental' and 'the most glorious instance'. Keble was, however, dissuaded from publishing the poem in which he allowed invocation directed towards the Blessed Virgin: 'So unforbidden may we speak/ An Ave to Christ's Mother meek;/ (As children with "good morrow" come/ To elders in some happy home).'

Among the writers of our own century, Canon Allchin limits his attention to the poets. Describing a stained glass window, the Welsh poet Euros Bowen speaks of Mary's form appearing 'like the brightest of flowers. . . a gentle virgin, like a heaven of snow. . ./ Fair swirling waters at Aberglasyn,/ Bilberries trailing their myrrh on the Berwyns'. 'The Virgin is a cup, a grail for the blood of the Spirit.' T.S. Eliot sees no end to the tragedies of the sea, 'Only the hardly, barely prayable/ Prayer of the one Annunciation'. Mary is the 'Lady, whose shrine stands on the promontory', on the boundary between earth and heaven.

The word to sum up these writers' attitude to Mary is 'love'. Members of the Roman Catholic communion, to which I belong, will find their devotion to Mary enriched by Canon Allchin's study.

Edward Yarnold s.j.

NOTES
1 A.M. Ramsey, *From Gore to Temple*, London (1960), p. 27.
2 *Acta Apostolicae Sedis*, 64 (1972), pp. 197-8.

Preface

This book was first published in 1984. It is now presented in a new and substantially enlarged edition. It had its origins more than twenty years ago in an invitation to lecture on the Anglican approach to Mariology in the ecumenical section of the Institut Catholique in Paris. I am grateful for the opportunity which was then given to me to think and read further on this subject. After many delays the book was at last finished under the hospitable roof of the abbey of Ste Marie du Mont in northern France. The prayers and friendship of the brethren did much to make its conclusion possible.

But though begun and ended in France the book itself is very English and very Anglican. It contains a study of a forgotten strand in the history of Anglican thought and devotion. Among the writers considered in it only Euros Bowen and Edwin Muir are not English and only Edwin Muir is not Anglican; and they both come from the British Isles. Because the intellectual history of Anglicanism is very little known even to Anglicans I have provided at the end a kind of dramatis personae, a list of the principal writers involved with an indication of their dates and character, in order to introduce others to some of the ramifications of our family tree.

The book is in the first place a study of the *place* of Mary in the Christian scheme of things rather than a study of her personality. The writers examined do not speculate much upon the actions, thoughts, and feelings of Mary. In this respect they mostly show great restraint and follow the example of the gospel narratives. They take their picture of her above all from St Luke. They see her as one in whom the Beatitudes are embodied. 'Blessed are the poor in spirit, the meek, the pure in heart.' They see her above all as a person of active and trusting faith and of free and courageous obedience. 'Blessed are those who hear the word of God and keep it.' They do not fail to reflect upon St Luke's remark that she kept all these things and pondered them in her heart. So they see her as a woman of deep and prayerful inwardness, as well as of an active loving concern. In these things too she stands in solidarity with the history of the people to whom she belongs. She is the daughter of Abraham, whose faith and obedience she follows. In these things she also stands in solidarity with the whole people of God through the two thousand years of Christian history.

But if they do not speculate much about her thoughts and feelings, they do reflect at length on her place in the scheme of redemption. Like the present Archbishop of Canterbury, they judge that 'it would be wrong . . . to push Mary to the circumference of the Christian story. Her place is in the centre.' They are unanimous in their view of her role in the mystery of the incarnation. The Word was made flesh and dwelt among us. Mary's role in this taking flesh, her free and personal consent, was absolutely vital, for God will not override human freedom. Moreover her maternal role speaks to us of the physical nature of this process. All our human life and therefore, on this understanding of things, all our divine life is mediated to us through the body, rooted in bodily functions in the ordinary processes of birth. These link us with all other living creatures and thus with the material world. As they ponder on this aspect of the incarnation, they begin to look into the God-bearing capacity not only of human life but of the whole creation. The material world, the world of plants and animals in all its fragility and exuberance, is touched by the divine and is shown to be capable of the divine. Let everything that has breath praise the Lord.

These thoughts are rooted in a sense of wonder and amazement and they issue in acts of praise and worship which make use of all the poetic capacities of human speech. This means that there is in these writers a preference for the poetic image over the intellectual concept. It does not mean, however, that the intellectual concept, the use of discursive and analytical reason, is simply abandoned. As we see in the case of Lancelot Andrewes, who stands at the root of this whole tradition, it is by the strict and rigorous use of our powers of reason that we can recognize the limits of reason and be led into more total and inclusive ways of knowing and speaking. Hence the language of prose constantly moves towards the language of poetry and song. To express the mystery we need paradox and metaphor as well as direct logical affirmation.

In this new and enlarged edition I have not altered the general shape of the book or the sequence of the chapters, though their numbering is altered. I have taken the opportunity throughout to adapt my style to contemporary sensibilities and in many places I have added new material. This is particularly the case in chapters five and six. Traherne takes a more central place than he did before. One of the reasons why the seventeenth-century section bulks large is that the works of most of the writers studied are difficult of access for the majority of readers. It has therefore been necessary to quote at length to give something of their flavour as well as their content. But although this is a fuller treatment of the subject than in the first edition, it is in no way meant to be exhaustive; particularly in the last section the writers are chosen as representative figures of a whole tradition which deserves much fuller and more systematic exploration.

In the late 1960s when this book was first contemplated, the themes which it tackles seemed decidedly outlandish. In the years which have passed since then the theological climate has changed greatly. To speak now of the place of the body in the Christian scheme of things, of the nature of the joy which should inform Christian worship, and of the rôle of Mary in the drama of salvation is less unexpected than it was in the late 1960s. We live at a time when there is a steadily increasing interest in prayer and spirituality and a growing sense that in the life of Christian faith we need to understand more of our poetic and intuitive capacities as well as our strictly rational ones. Everywhere there is new concern for the appreciation and articulation of the hidden feminine element in the Christian tradition. Everywhere too there is a concern to find ways of rediscovering the sacredness of the earth, for in many different situations people have suddenly realized how fragile and vulnerable our planet is. All these are themes which are considered in this book. It is my hope that these pages may be of help in bringing old and new light to bear on the consideration of the questions with which our time so urgently confronts us.

I

The Senses . . .
Our Deliverance

It is of the very nature of the Christian gospel, and indeed of all Christian praying and thinking, that it is at once particular, concerned with this place and this time, anchored in the specificity of things, and at the same moment full of eternity and mysteriousness. It is a meeting place where something of earth encounters something of heaven. We shall not understand it unless we see both sides of the antinomy; that it is precisely not abstract and generalized, but specific and only thus universal.

This sacramental or symbolic quality in Christian thinking and living has tended to be lost to sight in recent centuries in the development of an intellectualized theology itself deeply influenced by the intellectual and spiritual development of the West since the Renaissance and the Reformation. This whole tendency has made for a separation between spirit and matter, mind and body, so that the body and the material world have become increasingly divorced from the realm of mind and spirit, and have been sometimes ignored and despised, and sometimes cultivated and worshipped as ends in themselves. In the last hundred years especially, we have sought to preserve an inner world of meaning and subjectivity, over against the threat of an outer world of vast, impersonal and mechanistic realities.

Everywhere at the present time there is a sense that this development has run its course; people are seeking to find new ways to put together worlds which have been too long separated. Indeed the very facts of our time, inner and outer alike, are forcing us to the discovery of a new wisdom. One of the central areas in this new discovery is the reaffirmation of the place of the body in our life as human beings. In medicine and psychology, in philosophy and theology alike, it is seen with new force that the human being forms a unity, not mind and matter, not soul and body, as two distinct entities, but a single reality of life, a human person in whom soul and body are at one. Human life, in its most 'spiritual', its most personal aspects, is lived in and through the body, and not apart from it. Knowing is a bodily function; not only in that union of man and woman in mutual giving which in Hebrew was called knowledge, but in all forms of knowing, which are in some degree personal and embodied. And though we cannot dispense with reason and consciousness, knowledge is something more than the conscious and rational activity of the mind alone. We know with the whole of ourselves.

This is pre-eminently true of the knowledge of God. If we can know God at all, it is with a knowledge in which the body and the senses participate. If we are to know the divine, our ears and eyes no less than our hearts and minds must be made apt to the perception of heavenly realities. There are many stirrings of this insight at the present time, and it is one of the places in which the voice of William Blake sounds with a particular and prophetic urgency. But Blake is not alone among the thinkers and seers of the first part of the nineteenth century to be aware of the deeper currents of the human spirit in his time. Coleridge in his own very different way, is being revealed as a thinker of no less prophetic power. And one of the greatest of Anglican theologians of the nineteenth century, one who combined the rôle of theologian and natural scientist, who wedded meticulous scholarship to visionary insight, F.J.A. Hort, already in the mid-nineteenth century was pointing to him in this connection. In his remarkable but little known essay on Coleridge of 1856, Hort writes:

> Philosophy has denied that it has anything to do with the knowledge of God, and is now being rapidly swallowed up by positivism and science militant, and ancient experience tells us of a yet lower deep. Yet when we shall seem to lie at the lowest point, we may perhaps be near the very highest *and the senses themselves may become the very instruments* of our deliverance. Then philosophy may begin afresh once more, as from its Ionic cradle; and the spirit of Coleridge, which seemed

to be aimlessly stooping over a buried past, will be found rich in prophecy for a living future.[1]

It will be part of the purpose of this book to furnish an indirect commentary on this packed and hermetic statement. It need hardly be said that when Hort speaks here of 'science militant', he is not arguing against the natural sciences in themselves. Had he not thought their development essential for the future of humankind, he would hardly have devoted so much of his own time to the study of them. Rather he is speaking of a militant 'scientism', which by denying the necessity of other forms of knowing and thinking than those employed in the investigation of material phenomena, or by seeking to assimilate all such other forms to itself, effectively destroys the very basis upon which it operates. Again, the reference to the pre-Socratic philosophers, while it may strike us as in a way prophetic of the interest which they have aroused in the present century, ought not to engage our attention too exclusively. What is essential is the conviction of Coleridge, that the whole content of a long process of development may be given in principle in its initial instant, and that the development of human knowledge and understanding is more like the unfolding and articulation of a single infinitely rich moment of vision, than a simple linear progression from one phase to another. In both cases, as Hort points out, it will be through the senses themselves that we may find our liberation, may become free again to live in a world which is not ultimately subject to meaninglessness and death.

For the body and the senses cannot be ignored in any serious reflection on the Christian mystery. The idea of incarnation indeed focuses our attention upon them from the outset. An older theologian than Hort, and a near contemporary of Blake, one of the few genuinely theological spirits in an age of little vision in the Church, wrote:

The Gospel commenced in an accommodation to man's animal exigencies which was as admirable as it was gracious. . . The Incarnation of the co-eternal Son, through which St John was enabled to declare what he and his fellow-Apostles 'had seen with their eyes, what they had looked upon and their hands had handled, of the Word of Life,' was, in the first instance, so

17

to consult human nature in its animal and sensitive capacity, as to give the strongest pledge that a dispensation thus introduced would, in every subordinate provision, manifest the same spirit and operate on the same principle.[2]

God's way of acting is all of a piece. He wills to be incarnate now no less than then. The incarnation of the co-eternal Son cannot be an isolated wonder. However we interpret its uniqueness, and all Christian tradition insists that in some sense it is unique, we cannot think of it as something of the past. It is, as Alexander Knox says, the source of a permanent admiration.

Here already the place of Mary within the Christian dispensation is clearly coming into view. God enters into the material world. He is present at the roots of humanity's affective, natural, bodily life. The fullness of the deity is revealed not only in the mind and speech of Jesus, but in his body, that which he took from us, that in which he is most at one with us. The most basic of human experiences, of needs and satisfactions, fulfilments and anxieties are the soil in which the divine is revealed and grows. Every human act, rooted in the material, animal order, part of the material world and sharing much with the animal creation, can yet become fully human, in becoming free and consciously realized, can indeed be known as a gift, discovered as a response of thanks to God, can be divine. Grace shines through, illuminates and transfigures the natural order in its totality, shows that it has a wholly unsuspected goal and destiny; for God has entered into the very processes of birth.

Here in classical Christian faith there is a very great affirmation of the goodness of the human, despite all its empirical disorder and decay. The human is capable of the divine. Through the gift of God, the divine life is rooted in the human, the human in the divine. And here precisely is the cause of great joy and amazement. For precisely in 'man's animal exigencies' the ultimate glory is revealed, just where we had least expected it. Hence everywhere in the Christian world where she is known, Mary's name is associated with joy. She is the joy of joys, the cause of our joy, the joy of all creation. Latin, Greek, Russian, Syriac all proclaim the same thing. In her there is a meeting of opposites, of God and humankind, of flesh and spirit, of time and eternity, which causes an explosion of joy, a kind of ecstasy. It is the joy which is known in human life, 'when

18

the opposites come together, and the genuinely new is born'.[3]

Christianity says much about suffering and sorrow, pain and grief, and the way forward through death to life, through separation to a final and ultimate unity. In a world such as ours it would not be of much use, if it were unable to confront these realities of suffering and separation. But this is not all that it has to say. The gospel can also speak of a joy and innocence, which if it is known fleetingly in this world is yet a true element in human experience. If at first we might be tempted merely to juxtapose these two visions, the vision of innocence and life, the vision of death and resurrection, deeper reflection will show that the two are most intimately connected, and that in this world the former is strangely dependent on the latter. Only in the light of the triumph of the cross can this world be seen as again touched by the divine glory. It is from the cross that joy has come into the world.

The great mosaic in the church of the Holy Wisdom in Istanbul speaks eloquently of this fact. It presents the figure of Christ, between that of the Baptist and the Virgin Mother. On the one side is the prophet, the face furrowed with grief, with the sorrow of this world, its experience of frustration, of not fulfilling the purpose for which it was created, yet looking with a hope, hardly won, towards the way of repentance, the way of newness of life. On the other side is the figure of Mary, in the purity and transparency of her human beauty, the transfiguration of that vision of the perfection of the human body which characterized ancient Greece. Both things are true, and both meet in the grave yet radiant majesty of the central figure of the Christ.

The same thing is to be seen again in the same city, once the queen of cities, the particular heritage of the Queen of heaven, in the mosaics of the church of Our Saviour in Chora. Here in the narthex and exonarthex are a whole series of brilliant and delicate representations of the birth and childhood of Mary, and of the birth and childhood of Jesus. They are a celebration of human love and tenderness, of the care of parents for their children, of the joy of children in the security of their parents' love, and they formed the ground, the basis for the further development of the mystery of the salvation of the human race which would have been unfolded in the mosaics of the central space of the church, but which are no longer in existence. Baptism, transfiguration, crucifixion, resurrection and ascension, all these things are rooted in the coming together of Joachim and Anna, or in the nurture of the infant Jesus. To stop at these first images would be to perceive only a part of the truth; to seek to omit them would be to misconceive the greater realities to which they lead on.

It has not been customary to speak in this way in theology, to make such use of mosaic and poetry as we shall do in this study. Can we take such things 'seriously' in a serious context? Is the knowing of an artist or a poet, serious knowing; can it tell us the truth, or is it mere imaginative fancy? It will be clear that for us, the power of vision, physical and imaginative, no less than intellectual, has its part to play in the work of theology. Not that the imagination is in some special way a divine faculty, or that it cannot be deceived. It shares with the reason our human condition of fallenness, and it can be deceitful in its own fashion. But if the work of theology is to have at its centre the texts of the Bible and the liturgy, then we must allow that the image will have a certain priority over the concept, for these texts are for the most part imagist rather than conceptual. This does not mean that conceptual thinking is not necessary, or that it can be simply replaced by a symbolical approach; still less does it mean that we can dispense with clarity and precision. The work of theology has need of all the clarity and accuracy which we can bring into it. But we shall recognize that in approach to the truth of God something more than simple accuracy is required. In some sense it is images and symbols which come first. It is concepts which elucidate and clarify them.

One of the outstanding poets of our time, Les Murray, has spoken about this in recent years in two remarkable essays on the subject of embodiment. Murray makes use of the terms Narrowspeak and Wholespeak to distinguish between two different modes of discourse, prosaic and poetic, and lying behind them, two different modes of perception. Wholespeak is for him a way of speaking which corresponds to the fullness of our human potential for consciousness, to the dreaming, intuitive capacities of the older levels of the brain, as well as to the waking discursive capacities of the forebrain. Narrowspeak is the way of discursive reason alone, analytic, calculating, carefully dispassionate. For Murray both levels of discourse are necessary to human life. It is dangerous for an individual if one level altogether eclipses the other. In our society as a whole, however, Narrowspeak has often been regarded as the principal if not the only vehicle for serious, objective discourse. It is part of the poet's task to help correct this imbalance.

In Murray's view of things a true poem occurs when thinking and dreaming are fused together into one. 'A poem, or any work of art, enacts this wholeness and draws us into it . . .' On this understanding, Wholespeak is 'properly integrated poetic discourse'. Discourse based 'on the supposed primacy or indeed exclusive sovereignty of daylight reason I call Narrowspeak. The former embraces all good poetry, including that of religion; the latter embraces most of the administrative discourse by which the world is ruled from day to day as well as most criticism.' Of course the writer recognizes that both forms are in their own way necessary to human life. But he would maintain that it is vital that we recognize a certain primacy in Wholespeak.

No less vital is it to recognize that the affirmations of Wholespeak involve the life of the body as well as the life of the intellect and the imagination, our dreaming and our thinking selves, as Murray calls them. All our intellectual and imaginative life is rooted in the body, without which there can be no human wholeness. To recognize this is to recognize something essential in our human capacity for relationship with God.

> God can reach us through any of the modes of our life, through our dream consciousness, through our waking intellect, though that is much more capable of resisting him, and through the vegetative life of our body, in which he may be most constantly present. He seems to reach us most easily in our wholeness or the opposite extreme in our disintegration; where we are most resistant to him is in the middle range of premature and temporary self-integration.[4]

In the light of such insights, it is not perhaps surprising that we shall be led in the course of this study to affirm that in our own century it has been the poets rather than the professional teachers of theology who have often fulfilled the true theological function, of speaking of the divine revealed in the human, of the human taken into the divine, of declaring the true nature of human life as sacramental, full of mysteriousness, a potentiality which it can

21

never fully contain or express. 'They declare, with a perpetual insistence, the mysteriousness of our present being . . . they take the side of faith and patience against the attractions of completeness and security and achievement and repose.'[5]

The words quoted speak, in their original context, of sacraments not of poets. Yet they are true of both, and are followed by a remarkable tribute from a late nineteenth-century theologian to an early nineteenth-century poet, in which the hierarchical order in the Church – for the writer, Francis Paget, was already a regius professor and later became a dean and a bishop – pays due respect to the prophetic or charismatic order. They are words which point to truths which the experience of our own century has only rendered more clear and evident.

It is given sometimes to a poet to sink a shaft, as it were, into the very depths of the inner life: to penetrate its secret treasuries, and to return, Prometheus-like, with a gift of fire and of light to men. The venturesome words that record such a moment of penetration and insight never lose their power; they seem to have caught something of the everlasting freshness of that world of which they speak: and one man after another may find in them, at some time of need or gladness or awakening, the utterance of thoughts which else he might have been too shy or too faint-hearted to acknowledge even to himself. There is such a splendid venture of courage for the truth's sake in those lines of Wordsworth which surely no familiarity can deprive of their claim to reverence and gratitude; the lines in which he tells us of his thankfulness

. . . for those obstinate questionings
Of sense and outward things,
   Fallings from us, vanishings;
   Blank misgivings of a creature
Moving about in worlds not realised,
High instincts before which our mortal nature
Did tremble like a guilty thing surprised.
   . . . those first affections,
Those shadowy recollections,
   Which, be they what they may,
   Are yet the fountain-light of all our day,

Are yet a master-light of all our seeing;
Uphold us, cherish, and have power to make
Our noisy years seem moments in the being
Of the eternal silence. . .'[6]

Very characteristically Wordsworth speaks here of two distinct yet closely connected things. There are 'the first affections, the shadowy recollections', the memory from before consciousness, the haunting sense of eternity and wholeness perceived in childhood, on the one side; and on the other side, there are the questionings, the misgivings of the adult world, the sense of fear, indeed the guilt before the infinite, which can open up within the fabric of our daily lives, and suddenly bestow on them an unexpected sense and meaning. These moments, these recollections, though in the deepest sense spiritual, indeed divine, are never, in Wordsworth, disincarnate or generalized. They are felt through the senses, known through sight and smell, through hearing and touch, rooted in the life of the body.[7] 'The moments of such visitation are', Paget continues, 'the supreme opportunities of a human soul, the crises of its tragedy. . . We rise and we live and grow and see by the right understanding and employment of such moments. . .', for in them we can find 'the disclosure, the assertion, the stepping forward of his presence who alone sustains our life, our thought, our love'.[8]

If, as Christian faith has always affirmed, it is in the man Jesus of Nazareth that we find the supreme disclosure, assertion, stepping forward of him who alone sustains our life, our thought, our love, then the person of the woman who was his mother, out of whom, bodily, he came, cannot but be a central theme of Christian reflection.

But how are we to approach this subject of the place and rôle of Mary? Even the approach to the question is full of perplexities. On the one hand there is the slender evidence in the New Testament writings, on the other the enormous burgeoning of Christian doctrine and devotion through the centuries. On the one hand there is the silence of Protestantism, sometimes respectful, sometimes indifferent, sometimes hostile, on the other hand the enormous, one might think disproportionate, volume of speculation on the part of the Roman Catholic theologians in the century which preceded Vatican II. Here is a question on which Christians have fought one

23

another and wounded one another. The very terms which they use have been hardened and falsified in the course of a polemic, in which insights given for the healing and restoration of human life have been used to defend and attack entrenched positions. Here is a question in which thought and feeling are both deeply involved, where no one who begins to reflect finds that he can be altogether neutral. How are Christians from different traditions to break the uneasy silence on this subject which too often reigns between them when they come together?

It might at first sight seem that the obvious place from which to begin is that which all Christians have in common, the gospels, the New Testament, the Bible as a whole.[9] For a variety of reasons, however, I shall not take that route, not least because this is most evidently one of the places where what Christians see in the biblical text depends to a large degree on their whole living experience of the Christian reality as it has been mediated to them in the Christian community to which they belong. Instead of beginning with the gospels I shall begin with tradition, and precisely with the tradition of my own Church, believing that here, as in other places, despite and through all its limitations, Anglicanism can open up a way into the fullness of Christian truth and understanding. I shall begin with our seventeenth-century theologians, men who stood in the life and faith of a community which was conscious both of its continuity with the Church of the centuries before the Reformation, and of its indebtedness to certain of the central affirmations of the Reformers, men who sought to enlarge and deepen that faith and life through a contact with the living tradition of the Fathers of the Church, particularly whose who lived before the split between East and West. I follow the method of the Church of England and appeal to the authority of 'the Scriptures as interpreted by the perpetual practice of God's Church', aware that such a large and general criterion will not give quick or easy solutions, but believing that in the end it may prove more satisfactory than other seemingly more attractive alternatives.

I appeal to the seventeenth century not only on account of the largeness of its own understanding of tradition, but also on account of a particular quality of its faith and thought. When in the 1920s one of the greatest poets, and in the older meaning of the word, one of the greatest theologians of our time announced his acceptance of the Christian faith, he did so in a volume called *For Lancelot Andrewes*. The title is not fortuitous. T.S. Eliot found in the sermons of Andrewes, as in the theology of Hooker, in the life of the family at Little Gidding, in the church building of Sir Christopher Wren, signs of a Catholicism which was not ignorant either of the Renaissance or of the Reformation, a tradition which, in that sense had already moved into the modern world and lived on our side of the gulf which separates us from the Middle Ages. It was a Catholicism which had taken humanism and criticism into itself, without being destroyed by them. 'A Catholicism *without* the element of humanism and criticism', Eliot wrote in that book, 'would be a Catholicism of despair.'[10]

Many of Eliot's contemporaries felt that this was the only Catholicism which was available, that the great universal life-giving affirmations of Christian faith could only be made on the basis of the acceptance of a clearly defined external and infallible authority. They sought accordingly to stifle their questions and their scepticism by an appeal to the authority of the central see of Western Christendom. Only since Vatican II has released within the Roman Catholic Church all the forces of a free and questioning Catholicism, has it been possible to measure both the strength and the weakness of that other more authoritarian version of the Roman tradition to which so many of them adhered, a version which can still exert an attraction on the fearful today. Eliot chose another way. He believed that, for him in England, another form of the Catholic tradition was open, one in which the authority of God's self-disclosure is mediated in a much greater variety of ways. In Andrewes, he wrote, we hear 'the voice of a man . . . who speaks with the old authority and the new culture'. In the theology of his school he found 'a determination to stick to essentials, that awareness of the needs of the times, the desire for clarity and precision in matters of importance, and the indifference to matters indifferent',[11] which seemed to him to indicate a balance of tradition which was necessary in his own times.

Still more, Eliot found in the religion of this period something of even greater value to his own faith; a faith which did not so much reject and suppress doubt, as carry its scepticism within itself. Recounting an incident which took place in Cambridge about the time of the publication of *For Lancelot Andrewes*, a friend of

Eliot writes: 'As we walked back through the empty courts in the small hours, Eliot made one comment which I always found very helpful in understanding his religious position. There was, he quietly observed, a great difference between the Marxists and himself, not only or merely in the content of his beliefs, but even more in the way in which they were held, "They seem so certain of what they believe. My own beliefs are held with a scepticism which I never even hope to be quite rid of".'[12] The friend who recounts the incident remarks on the light which it throws on Eliot's relationship to the Anglican seventeenth-century poets, to Donne and Herbert in particular, in whom there is the constant interplay between faith and questioning. One might also note here one of the points of affinity between Eliot and his contemporary Charles Williams whose own burning faith contained within itself precisely this vein of questioning and criticism.

Such a faith is in no sense a half-hearted or temporizing thing. Nothing could be clearer than that, both in Eliot's life and in his writing. One is tempted to qualify as heroic his adherence to the strictness of Christian faith in a society and milieu so wholly unsympathetic to it – while his writings, above all the *Four Quartets*, contain an exposition of the depths of the tradition of Christian spirituality and theology which is unequalled in our century. Rather it is a faith which recognizes our hopeless ignorance before the mysteries of God, and does not pretend to find answers when it has not got them. It recognizes at every point 'the mysteriousness of our present being'. It 'takes the side of faith and patience against the attractions of completeness and security and achievement and repose'. It is a factor in the Anglican tradition which makes for a certain tentativeness and humility before the affirmations of theology and which corresponds very closely to the apophatic elements, the awe and the reserve, which characterize the teaching of the great Fathers of East and West alike. This characteristic does not imply any refusal of knowledge, any turning away from God's gift of himself. It is rooted rather in an experience of the limitations of human language and human concepts, and expresses a humility before the immensity of the divine.

This tradition has, moreover, a further quality which is of equal significance. It recognizes that our approach to God must be complex, multiple, if it is to take in the whole of our being, and in any way correspond to the fullness of God's revelation of himself. God in his approach to us will speak and act in a variety of ways. It will, therefore, distrust any theological system which leans so wholly on transcendence as to emphasize redemption and revelation to the exclusion of creation and nature. It will be as uneasy with any system which tends wholly to immanence, and which loses the specificity of revelation in some general scheme of evolutionary development. In the words of an eminent Anglican theologian of our century, commenting on the theological method of Richard Hooker, 'God as the ultimate reality must be approached by many paths; through the witness of nature and of the religious impulse, as well as through the moral conscience, through each and all of these as well as through the special revelation which he has given us. To each of these too we must allow its own method, only seeking to show how in the end they corroborate one another.'[13] Here is the root of the attempt to differentiate between things essential, and things less essential, between what is of central significance and what of ancillary worth.

It will be our contention that we shall have need of all these qualities in our approach to the vast and sometimes perplexing phenomenon of Marian devotion and reflection, of holy place and pilgrimage, of apparition and locution. We must not, of course, ignore the witness of Scripture, for unless the whole development is in some sense anchored in the heart of the Christian mystery, then it must be condemned as at least irrelevant to the intent of God's act in Jesus Christ. But at the same time we shall not dismiss, as without any value, 'the witness of nature and of the religious impulse', so that while we may scrutinize carefully those places where devotion to the Mother of God seems to bring Christianity most close to other religions, we shall by no means reject them out of hand. The Word of God by whom all things were made, has left his imprint upon all our life and thought, not least upon our strivings after the divine. Above all we shall have need of a respectful agnosticism, neither too hasty to accept or refuse, what at times may seem strange, or even maybe repellent, but rather seeking to see how it relates to the central and amazing affirmation of faith made by all Christians, that God was in Christ and that in man the fullness of the divinity dwelt bodily.

It was in the opening years of Vatican II that Charles Moeller, of Louvain, a Roman Catholic theologian who was to have a

27

considerable influence in the Council's deliberations, published a book on the way in which the faith should be presented in the second half of the twentieth century. One of the issues which he discussed was the position of Mary. He was not at all unaware of the tendencies toward exaggeration and disproportion which had marked a good deal of Mariology in the years since Vatican I. It was in this context that he wrote,

> It would seem that the Mariological mysteries tend, just as Mary did in her earthly life, to efface themselves in the light which comes to them from beyond, and with which they shine. They seem to efface themselves for they show us how to go beyond them, not doubtless in order to forget them, but so that thanks to the divine light with which they are filled, we may enter more intimately into the mysteries of Christ, of the Spirit, of the Church, and of the end of the ages... And yet, we know that these Marian mysteries which seem content to gravitate around the greater mysteries, are mysteriously the source of these mysteries themselves. If everything comes from the initiative of God in Jesus Christ, nonetheless it remains true that without Mary the Word could not become incarnate; there is the unfathomable mystery of the love of God which respects and re-creates his creation to such a point that he has as it were need of the fiat of Mary in order that the incarnation may take place.[14]

It is from such a perspective that this book has been written and is offered to the attention of Christians of all Churches and of none in the hope that it may remove some unnecessary fears and misapprehensions.

NOTES

1 F.J.A. Hort in 'Coleridge', *Cambridge Essays* (1856)
2 Alexander Knox, *Remains*, vol. i, p. 330
3 Monica Furlong, source unknown
4 Les Murray, *The Paperbark Tree: Selected prose* (Manchester 1992) pp. 260-3 and 265-6. Les Murray is himself a Roman Catholic. The essay 'Embodiment and Incarnation', from which these quotations are taken, was published in Sydney in 1987 in an Anglican-based periodical.

5 Francis Paget, in Charles Gore (ed.), *Lux Mundi* (1889), 'Sacraments', p. 429

6 Ibid., pp. 429-30

7 Cf. Alec King, *Wordsworth and the Artist's Vision: an Essay in Interpretation* (1966)

8 Op. cit., p. 431

9 For an eminently balanced presentation of this subject in the light of Scripture and the early tradition of the Church, written from an Anglican viewpoint, see John de Satgé, *Mary and the Christian Gospel* (1976)

10 T.S. Eliot, *For Lancelot Andrewes* (1928), p. 140

11 Ibid., p. 17

12 From 'Mistah Kurtz: He Dead' by H.S. Davies, in Allen Tate (ed.), *T.S. Eliot: The Man, his Work* (1967)

13 L.S. Thornton, *Richard Hooker: A Study of his Theology* (1924), p. 104

14 Charles Moeller, *Evangelisation et Mentalité Moderne, p.137*

Part One

The Seventeenth-Century Witness

2

'This We are to Hold':
Lancelot Andrewes

'God was in Christ reconciling the world to himself.' The doctrine of the incarnation, as the act of God by which reconciliation is brought about, and humankind and God are united, was at the heart of the theology of seventeenth-century Anglicanism. Any consideration of the rôle and person of Mary has to be seen always and only in relation to that great primordial mystery of God's love, and it is in this perspective that the question is viewed by the Anglican writers of this period. 'And for as much as there is no union of God with man without that mean between both which is both, it seemeth requisite that we first consider how God is in Christ, then how Christ is in us, and how the sacraments do serve to make us partakers of Christ. In other things we may be more brief, but the weight of these requireth largeness.'[1]

With these words Richard Hooker stands back from his detailed examination of the Puritan objections to the Book of Common Prayer and introduces his magisterial discussion of the doctrine of Christ. It is an exposition which recapitulates and reaffirms the teaching of the Fathers and the early Councils, and which established, at the foundation of the Anglican theological tradition, the inseparable links between the doctrine of Christ, of the Church and the sacraments. It need hardly be said that the whole of this argument in Hooker, and throughout this period, is carried on in the terms which had been employed in the ancient Church; that is to say, in terms of the union of the two natures, human and divine, in the one person of Jesus Christ, the Son of God. These are not necessarily terms which come easily to us. But they represent not only the thought but also the prayer and experience of many centuries. It may well be the task of contemporary theology to see whether, with a different approach, the same truth may be expressed in other and more accessible phrases. Indeed, if Christendom were united, why should it not be that the Spirit of God would guide us into new formulations no less valid than the old? But we do well to recognize that the traditional categories, stiff though they may sometimes seem to us, express a fullness and balance of faith and insight which is easily betrayed, and that they are therefore not to be lightly laid aside. In seeking to see what they can mean for us in relation to our themes of celebration, of the Mother of the Lord, and the redemption of the body, we may get a new glimpse of the richness of the mystery which they express.

The term *Theotokos*, Mother of God, though defined by the Council of Ephesus, is not used explicitly by Hooker in his treatise *The Laws of Ecclesiastical Polity*. But the faith which the term intended to express and to safeguard is the faith which he is expounding, so that we cannot imagine that he would have rejected it. As to the belief that the life of God touches the whole of us, body and soul alike, there can be no question in his writings. As L.S. Thornton remarks, Hooker's is 'a religion of flesh and blood, of Eucharist and Resurrection', an expression of the tradition which 'comes down to us from the Fourth Gospel, through Irenaeus, Tertullian and the Greek Fathers'.[2] In this connection Hookers' stress upon the true humanity of Christ is particularly important. 'Doth any man doubt', Hooker writes, 'that even from the flesh of Christ our very bodies do receive that life which shall make them glorious at the latter day, and for which they are already accounted parts of his blessed Body? Our corruptible bodies would never live the life they shall live, were it not that here they are joined with his body, which is incorruptible, and that his in ours is a cause of immortality. . . Christ is therefore both as God and as man, that true Vine whereof we both spiritually and corporally are branches.'[3] This union bodily is not to be thought of in crudely physical terms; but it is to be seen as an expression of the faith that even now the healing power of God is at work through our whole nature. This faith is vital for Hooker. And in this work, the sacrament of the Eucharist has its part to play. 'In the words of endless import', to quote Paget commenting on this section, Hooker affirms ' "there ensueth a kind of transubstantiation in us, a true change of both soul and body, an alteration from death to life."' As Paget notes, these words rest directly on those of Irenaeus, in the second century: 'As bread from the earth receiving the invocation of God is no longer common bread, but the Eucharist, consisting of two things, an earthly and a heavenly; so our bodies also receiving the Eucharist are no longer corruptible, having the hope of the Resurrection.' 'Alike in us and in the Sacrament,' Paget concludes, 'the powers of the world to come invade the present and already move towards the victory which shall be hereafter.'[4]

We are here already at a stand, not knowing what to feel or think in face of such exalted affirmations about the nature of humanity made by Christian thinkers of such widely separated times and places. Certainly, with Jeremy Taylor we may exclaim, 'This great and glorious mystery is the honour and glory of man', or with Lancelot Andrewes, 'This being beyond the rules and reach of all reason is surely matter of astonishment. "This it is said, saith St Chrysostom, casteth me into an ecstasy and maketh me imagine of our nature some great matter, I cannot well express what." Thus it is: it is the Lord, let him do what seemeth good in his own eyes.'[5]

The exposition of the Christian faith contained in Lancelot Andrewes's Ninety-six Sermons, preached year by year before the royal court at the great feasts of Christmas, Easter and Whitsun was to become one of the foundation stones of Anglican theology. It constitutes a magisterial unfolding of the richness and coherence of the Christian tradition, demonstrating at every point the relation of one doctrine to another, the necessity of each part to make up the whole. But these intensely theological sermons always have a practical end. They are intended to carry us out beyond ourselves, either into service of our neighbour, or into the love and worship of God. In this as in other things, Andrewes speaks in the manner of the Fathers. His teaching reflects that sober drunkenness of which they speak; by the use of the utmost power of reason going beyond the rules and reach of all reason.

In his study of Andrewes's theology as revealed in his sermons, Nicholas Lossky insists on the quality at once practical and mystical, at once rational yet reaching beyond reason, which characterizes these sermons. It is a characteristic which has its origins in that initial response of astonishment and wonder before the divine mystery which is to be found throughout Andrewes's work. Andrewes always underlines this element of mystery in God's revelation of himself in Christ. As Lossky points out, 'Andrewes never develops any doctrine for the love of abstract theological speculation; with him theology is manifest as essentially mystical, in the sense that any formulation of Christian teaching is only of value for the practical implications it must necessarily have in the spiritual life which all the time leads toward union with God.'6

But in doing this Andrewes always respects the rôle that the intellect plays in moving toward the mystery. His sermons are immensely learned and carefully reasoned. He does not underestimate the value of analytical argument, nor the significance of careful historical inquiry. But these things are not for him an end in themselves. He uses reason to bring us to the point where we have to acknowledge the limitations of reason. 'With him understanding must go to the very limits of its competence, in order to establish what could be called the mystery's terms of approximation, which allow one to contemplate its fullness in a recognition, founded on experience, of the limits of human reason.'7 Here we find that poetic images, because of their manifold and flexible quality, their capacity to hold together in one different aspects of truth which are apparently logically incompatible with one another, have a certain primacy over concepts. It is of course vital here to recognize that the Bible often speaks in this language of poetic imagery. Speaking of the Christmas sermons, Lossky points out how passages of rigorous intellectual exposition modulate into paragraphs in which the language of images comes to the fore. 'After the rigorous exposition which is addressed essentially to the reason . . . the preacher awakes the attention, the interest, and the participation of his hearer by provoking a wider apprehension of his part in responding to the incarnation, an apprehension at once sensuous and intellectual, founded on the indissoluble unity which he creates between verbal parallelism and intellectual paradox, which at one stroke transcends the confines of the intellect and brings the hearer face to face with a vision in which he can only contemplate simultaneously several terms that logically either succeed one another or exclude one another. The type of apprehension to which he is here making appeal is naturally comparable to the apprehension of a poem.'8

36

In this developed methodology of Andrewes's preaching, which Lossky compares with that to be found in Byzantine hymnody, we have one of the principle roots of the theological quality of much seventeenth-century poetry and of the poetic quality of much of the Anglican preaching of the period. For all their differences Herbert, Vaughan, and Traherne are all indebted to this method, as are the preachers whose work is considered in this book; evidently so in the case of Mark Frank, less obviously in the case of Jeremy Taylor. In them no less than in him we see something of this interaction and fusion of intellect and imagination which gives its distinctive character to the religious writing of this age.

This capacity to go beyond reason is illustrated by the passage from Andrewes quoted above, with its characteristic allusion to John Chrysostom. But what is it in particular which has caught Andrewes's attention? It is the implications of the mystery of the incarnation for the position of humankind within the whole hierarchy of created being which strikes him and which carries him from discursive thought to the silence of amazement. The sermon in which it occurs is based on the text 'For surely it is not with angels that he is concerned but with the descendants of Abraham'. Here is the comparison which the preacher is enforcing. The angels, he declares, 'in everything else, above and before us; in this beneath and behind us. And we unworthy, wretched men that we are, above and before the Angels, the Cherubim, the Seraphim and all the Principalities and Thrones in this dignity.'[9] We shall have later to consider what this comparison with angels means in relation to the traditional belief in the incarnation. Here let us simply register the fact that Andrewes is taking up a thread in the tradition which has particular relevance to the person of Christ's Mother, who in the worship of the Orthodox Church is constantly referred to as 'more honourable than the Cherubim, and incomparably more glorious than the Seraphim'. Whatever else these words say, they are evidently an expression of the intimacy with which God and humanity come together in Christ, and of the infinite distance which has been overcome in order to create that intimacy.

The reference to Mary is made explicitly by Andrewes in a later sermon, on the text of Galatians 4:4–5. 'When the time was fully come, God sent forth his Son, born of woman, born under the law, to redeem those who were under the law, so that we might receive

the adoption of sons.' Here he uses the sermon to expound the
union of the two natures in Christ, the coming together of human
and divine, of eternity and time.

> And so have we here now in one both twain His natures. 'God
> sent his Son' – there his divine: 'made of a woman' – here
> his human nature. That, from the bosom of his Father before
> all worlds; this, from the womb of his mother in the world.
> So that as from eternity God his Father might say that verse
> of the Psalm *Filius meus es Tu, hodie genui Te,* 'Thou art
> my Son, this day have I begotten Thee', so 'in the fullness
> of time' might the Virgin his Mother no less truly say, *Filius
> meus es Tu, hodie peperi Te,* 'Thou art my Son, this day have
> I brought thee into this world.'
>
> And here now at this word 'made of a woman', he beginneth
> to concern us somewhat. There groweth an alliance between
> us; for we also are made of a woman. And our hope is, as he
> will not be confounded, to be counted *inter natos mulierum;* no
> more will he be [confounded], saith the Apostle, to say *in medio
> fratrum* 'to acknowledge us his brethren'. And so by this time
> he groweth somewhat near us.[10]

There are two things here which call for our notice. First,
the coincidence of the two 'todays', on which Andrewes speaks at
length in this and other sermons. In the incarnation, time reaches a
certain fullness and, in some way, is taken up into eternity. There
is a union here of human life which passes away, with God's life
which does not pass away. Something eternal is realized in time.
Time is fulfilled in being transcended. There is an intersection
of the timeless with time. And this, which is supremely true of the
incarnation itself, is also true of all those moments in which
the incarnation is recalled, and made present again. It is true
in a particular way of the times when the Church comes
together to celebrate and recall these things in worship and
thanksgiving. Here is a clue as to the nature of liturgy and of
celebration which we shall find worked out in many other places.

The other point which concerns us here, and which leads us
further on, is Andrewes's insistence that it is in Christ's sharing our

human birth that he comes close to us, is gradually brought into proximity with us, and makes an 'alliance' with us. This is not some diplomatic contract. It is more like an alliance of families, made by marriage. By it, we find that we are 'advanced' beyond anything that we could have imagined. Herein, as Andrewes will underline, is love: Christ's love which draws us up to be where he is.

The same thoughts are to be found in another of the nativity sermons, no. xi, preached on the text from Psalm 85, 'Mercy and Truth are met together, Righteousness and Peace have kissed each other. Truth shall spring out of the earth, and Righteousness shall look down from heaven.'[11] This sermon has lying behind it the first of St Bernard's sermons on the Feast of the Annunciation, which employs the same text. It is interesting as an example of the way in which Andrewes uses not only the earlier Fathers as authoritative speakers for the tradition, but is prepared also to advance into the Latin Middle Ages in order to build up his picture of the fullness of the faith. For this is a sermon about fulfilment, about the conjunction of apparent opposites, about a meeting between parties which have been too long separated. 'Truth being now born of our nature, it will never, we may be sure, be against our nature; being come of the earth, it will be true to his own country; being made man, will be for man now all he can.' The link is established, we are all of one party. For Andrewes of course interprets the Psalm verse as a prophecy of the incarnation.

> The Truth, this he who declared 'I am the Truth', the earth, what is that but the flesh of man? And as the truth fits his nature, so doth earth man. Of whom God, 'earth thou art' (Gen. 3:19), to whom the Prophet thrice over, 'Earth, hear the word of the Lord' (Jer. 22:20); by whom the wise man, *Quid superbis?* 'Why should the earth be proud' (Ecclus. 10:19) *Germinet terra Salvatorem,* 'Let his earth bring forth a Saviour' – be the *terra promissionis,* the Blessed Virgin, who was in this the land of promise. So was this very place applied by Irenaeus in his time, who touched the Apostles' times; so by Lactantius; so by St Hierom and St Augustine. Those four meet in this sense, as do the four in the text. *Quid est veritas de terra orta? Est Christus de faemina natus? Quid est Veritas? Filius Dei. Quid terra? Caro nostra.*

'What the truth? Christ. What the earth? Our flesh.' In those words they find this feast all.'[12]

This interpretation of the Blessed Virgin as 'the good earth', 'the land of promise', which, as we have already suggested, is of great significance, is clearly of some special importance to Andrewes also. He draws out four witnesses from among the Fathers, and insists upon the antiquity of the first of them, as of one who links us with the age of the apostles. Andrewes has a liking for citing four witnesses from the tradition, as we shall see again. It was the number of the Evangelists, the primary witnesses to the events of the incarnation, it was the number of the first four Ecumenical Councils. It was for him a number which spoke of completeness and assurance.

And in the text four different attributes have met: Peace and Mercy on the one side, Righteousness and Truth on the other. Andrewes pictures the coming together of the apparent opposites in the birth of Christ, who rises out of the good earth, the land of promise, the Blessed Virgin.

And here again he sees a reconciliation of his eternal generation, and this his birth in time. 'For *orta est,* it is double; therefore *de terra* is well added. Another *ortus* he had *de Caelo*; to wit, His heavenly Divine nature which as "the day sprung from on high", and He in regard of it called *oriens* by Zachary in the New Testament (Luke 1:78). But this here is *de terra*; for the word properly signifies "the shooting forth of a sprig out of the ground", and he in regard of this *ortus* called "the Branch" by Zachary in the Old (Zech. 3:8).'

As the sermon continues so we see more of what is involved in the coming together of these four virtues. For Andrewes their conjunction corresponds to a fourfold pattern which can be found in creation as well as in redemption. It speaks of the necessity of completeness if we are to receive God's gift of life. It speaks of a continuing quality which should mark the whole development of the Christian life, personal as well as corporate. There is a fullness which needs to be maintained. 'For as this meeting made Christianity first; so there is nothing mars it, but the breaking it off again; no greater bane to it, than the parting of these.' And he goes on with emphasis,

Set this down then: Christianity is a meeting: one cannot meet, two there must be and they may. But it is not a meeting of two, but of two with two: so, no less than four. . . . And as it is a meeting, so a cross meeting, of four virtues that seem to be in a kind of opposition (as hath been noted). No matter for that. They will make the better refraction; the cool of one allay the heat, the moist of one temper the drought of the other. The soft virtues need to be quickened; the more forward to be kept from *altum sapere*. So are the elements of which are our bodies, so are the four winds of which our breath doth consist, which gives us life. And these in the text have an analogy or correspondence with the elements observed by the ancients; truth corresponds with the solid earth, peace with the running streams, mercy with the air we breathe, righteousness with the devouring fire.[13]

Here are themes which will recur in other places in our study of this subject, as we come to reflect further on the way in which the incarnation implies a constant meeting of apparent opposites. For Andrewes this point is of special importance. It is, he maintains, the very essence of heresy to fail to recognize this thing, but instead to take the part for the whole, to accept one truth without its complementary opposing truth. Again he affirms,

Christianity is a meeting, and to this meeting there go *pia dogmata*, as well as *bona opera*, righteousness as well as truth. Err not this error than to single out any (as it were) in disgrace of the rest; say not, one will serve the turn, what should we do with the rest of the four;. . . The truth is, sever them, and farewell all; take any one from the rest and it is as much as the whole is worth. For (as Bernard well observed) *non sunt virtutes si separentur*, upon their separation they cease to be virtues. . . Entertain them then all four; 1) Hope in Mercy; 2) faith in Truth; 3) fear of Righteousness; 4) love of Peace. . . O how loving a knot! how by all means to be maintained! how great a pity to part it![14]

Commenting on this sermon Nicholas Lossky draws out its Marian implications.

In the person of the Virgin, humanity, the 'flesh', co-operates actively in the incarnation of the Word of God. Conceiving

41

the Word of God by the Holy Spirit, she provides the place of this birth and this reconciliation of the four attributes. Now, if the event is unique in history, it is at the same time destined to be continued in Christianity in the person of each Christian:

'For I ask, did this hold, did this meet only in Christ? Do they not in Christianity likewise? Yes, there too. With Christ came Christianity; look, what in his birth now, in the new birth of everyone that shall be the better by it, even the same meeting of the very same virtues all.'

The new birth of everyone, a traditional expression for baptism, will soon be picked up in another form, more continuous in the Christian life. Indeed, the meeting in each believer of truth and mercy requires a condition: the truth of the confession of sins... Like the Virgin then, the Christian is called to give birth to the truth and to co-operate with his own salvation by encouraging the meeting of the divine attributes.[15]

For Andrewes the conjunction of the four qualities of truth, righteousness, mercy and peace will also lead us into the way of reconciliation and unity within the Church.

Mercy leads to truth and the knowledge of it; and truth to righteousness, and the practice of it; and righteousness to peace, and the ways of it – 'guides our feet first into the way of peace'. And such a way shall there always be, do all the controversy-writers what they can, a fair way agreed upon all sides, questioned by none, in which whoso orders his steps aright 'may see the salvation of our God'. Even the way here chalked out before us; to show mercy and speak truth; do righteousness and follow peace. And by this rule proceeding in the points whereto we are come already, even those truths wherein we are otherwise minded would in due time be revealed unto us.[16]

On this Lossky comments, 'Theology and life are inseparable, there is no orthodoxy without orthopraxy. Christianity demands the four virtues, just as Christ possessed nature, person, body and soul, and man cannot exist without the four elements, earth, water, air and fire.'[17]

Already in this sermon Andrewes has taken us into the consequences which come from the initial moment of incarnation, and has begun to investigate the thought of our being united with Christ as members of his body nourished and built up by his life. Before we examine these consequences further it is necessary to see a little more fully what is involved in the doctrine of the incarnation as to the person of the Mother of the Lord. In view of the fact that in his sermons Andrewes says quantitatively very little about her, it is remarkable how much he manages to say in these passages which we are about to examine from the Ninth Sermon for Christmas Day, on the text of Isaiah 7:14, 'Behold a virgin shall conceive and bear a son, and shall call his name Immanuel.' In them he touches the heart and core of the Church's devotion to Mary.

First we shall see how he stresses that here is something which goes beyond reason, and yet takes reason up into itself, then how he underlines that this is something where the power of God and the faith of humanity are altogether active in the creation of a new and paradoxical reality in which the opposites come together, and reconciliation takes place. And this faith, he insists, is not merely passive, it also contributes to the new thing which comes to birth.

> But I hold ever best to let everything rest upon his own base or bottom; natural upon reason, supernatural upon faith. And this is supernatural; in which *tota ratio facti est in potentia facientis*, 'the power of the doer is the reason of the thing done.' God is the doer, *Cujus dicere est facere*, 'to whom it is as easy to do it as to say it.' As the Angel concluded, so do I, 'With God is nothing impossible.' And that of Christ's, 'To faith all things are possible.' And here are both. And where they meet, they make no less a miracle than *Mater* and *Virgo*, or *Deus* and *Homo* – even *fides* and *ratio*. And this, for *Virgo concipiet*.'[18]

From this initial statement, Andrewes goes on to work out what is involved in this act of conception.

> This we are to hold; to conceive is more than to receive. It is so to receive as to yield somewhat of our own also. A vessel is not

43

said to conceive the liquor that is put into it. Why? Because it yieldeth nothing from itself. The Blessed Virgin is, and therefore is because she did. She did both give and take. Give of her own substance whereof his body was framed; and take or receive power from the Holy Ghost, whereby was supplied the office and the efficacy of the masculine seed. This is *concipiet*.[19]

We are aware by the very formula with which the preacher introduces this discussion, that it is for him a point of some importance. 'This we are to hold.' As much as to say, 'this we have received, this we must hand on.' Indeed, he quotes from Hilary, Gregory Nazianzen, Gregory the Great, and Bernard to show that this position is not a fancy of his own. Again we see the citing of four witnesses. Furthermore, Andrewes is conscious here of touching upon a point which was contested both by ancient and contemporary heretics. 'And this word is the bane of divers heresies. That of the Manichee that held, He had no true body. That had been, *virgo decipiet*, not *concipiet*; not – conceive Him, but deceive us. And that the Valentinian, revived lately in the Anabaptist, that held He had a true body, but made in Heaven and sent into her. That has been *recipiet* but not *concipiet*, received him she had, conceived him she did not.'[20]

If the former heresy is one which seems unfamiliar to us, the reverse is true of the second even though it is not put in precisely these terms. In schemes of theology which think to safeguard the transcendence and priority of God by denying any true reciprocity on the part of humankind, we have often heard of an activity of God which comes '*senkrecht von oben*', straight down from above without any contribution whatsoever from the human side, and which therefore can find no place for Christ's Mother either in thought or devotion. The heroic attempts made in the earlier period of Protestant neo-Orthodoxy, in works like Nygren's *Agape and Eros*, to deny the very possibility that human beings can love God look curiously artificial and unreal when seen in the light of a larger view of Christian thinking and experience. God's love for us is not in word or tongue, but in deed and truth. It enters into our flesh. To deny the mystery of the transformation which this works in humanity is not to magnify but to deny the power and reality of this love. As Karl Barth so clearly saw in his later writings, we do not truly exalt God, by seeking to depress humanity, made in his image. Nor can there be any real relationship of love unless human beings are able to love in return him by whom they find themselves to be loved.

And this is precisely the point which Andrewes here makes. He does not, as he very properly might have done, draw out from his *concipiet*, the thought about Mary, that she 'gives of her own substance', to the moment of incarnation, so that the divine truly appears in human form, a form with features which he had taken from her. He does not here reflect how much this tells us not only about Mary, but about everyone who seeks to make a free response of love to the divine initiative and thereby gives 'of his own substance', that the divine epiphany may take place. Others would do that later. He turns at once to what it says about the love of God, the primal, underlying reality which alone makes sense of, alone makes possible any movement of human love in response.

From which his conceiving we may conceive his great love to usward. Love, not only condescending to take our nature upon him, but to take it by the same way and after the same manner that we do, by being conceived. That, and no other better beseeming way... This sure is matter of love; but came there any good to us by it? There did. For our conception being the root as it were, the very groundsill of our nature; that he might go to the root and repair our nature from the very foundation, thither he went; that what had been there defiled and decayed by the first Adam, might by the second be cleaned and set right again. That had our conception been stained, by him therefore, *primum ante omnia*, to be restored again. He was not idle all the time he was an embryo – all the nine months he was in the womb; but then and there he even ate out the core of corruption that cleft to our nature and us, and made both us and it an unpleasing object in the sight of God.

And what came of this? We that were abhorred by God, *filii irae* was our title, were by this means made beloved in him. He cannot, we may be sure, account evil of that nature, that is now become the nature of his own son – his now no less than ours ... This honour is to us by the dishonour of him; this the good by Christ an embryo.[21]

He not only took our nature, but took it 'by the same way and after the same manner that we do'. He went to its very root, its groundsill. A dimension of the meaning of the incarnation is opened up here, which needs further exploration. We know more clearly than Andrewes did, the links which bind human conception to animal conception; the immensely long processes of evolution which in some way the human embryo recapitulates in the first stages of its development. All this was part of God's patience, all this was in some way assumed. For us, the womb will speak not only of the first and pre-conscious period of the individual's life, but also of all those mysterious areas which lie below and around the centre of our consciousness, areas which are still so little explored, and which still hold for us so much of terror, as well as of amazement. 'Thither he went.' When we look out from the island of consciousness into the surrounding sea of the unconscious, we find, as a twentieth-century poet puts it, swimming among 'the sea-beasts and archetypal monsters . . . the Easter-fish'; and as the sun of righteousness arises over the land, 'shedding his true, saving healthful and fruitful light', it penetrates even 'into the depths of the intractable sea, transfiguring the sea-monsters into servants for himself'.[22] It was an adage of the early Christian thinkers that what had not been assumed by God, could not be healed. But, as they argued, our whole nature has been healed, therefore there is nothing in it that was not assumed. The argument holds good today; the only difference is that we have a different, and in some respects larger, understanding of that which was assumed.

And, what is more, all that was done and all that is seen in this initial moment of incarnation is of universal import. It sheds its healing light back into the past. As Andrewes says in another sermon, quoting Pope Leo,

'the joy of it went back up to the ages past, even to Abraham's time, two thousand years and more before ever it came'.[23]

It is to be at work throughout the centuries of the future. All people are touched by it. All people are called to be reborn, to find themselves and so to grow as children of a divine and heavenly Father.

The Virgin's womb, however, is not the only place of birth.

There are also the waters of the font, which also bring forth new life. Nor is it only the first disciples who have seen with their eyes and handled with their hands. To us also the Word of life has made himself perceptible by the senses, given himself in his Body and his Blood, in a mystery, the hidden reality of the Eucharist. The sacraments, too, Andrewes tells us, are involved in the mystery of the incarnation, in the meaning of the name Emmanuel, which says that God is with us.

> 'With us' – to make us that to God, that he was this day to man. And this indeed was the chief end of his being 'with us'; to give us a *posse fieri*, a capacity, 'a power to be made the sons of God', by being born again of water and of the Spirit'; for *Originem quam sumpsit ex utero Virginis posuit in fonte Baptismatis*, 'the same original that himself took in the womb of the Virgin to usward, the same hath he placed for us in the fountain of Baptism to Godward'. Well therefore called the womb of the Church *sustoichon* to the Virgin's womb, with a power given it of *concipiet et pariet filios* to God. So his being conceived and born the Son of man doth conceive and bring forth (*filiato, filiationem*), our being born, our being the sons of God. His participation of our human, our participation of His Divine nature.[24]

The marvellous interchange which the incarnation brings about could not be more clearly expressed; his descent into our human life that we might be raised into the divine life. Nor could the significance of the great initial act of baptism be more strongly indicated, with the quotation from Pope Leo, which reminds us that the Church also is mother, with a maternity which stems from the motherhood of Mary. This is not an isolated passage in Andrewes's teaching. The same doctrine recurs at Easter and Whitsun as well. As the Fathers constantly say: God became man, in order that man might become God. He does not tire of driving home the message. This is the full scope of his faith. So in the third sermon for Whitsun he writes: 'The Holy Ghost is the Alpha and Omega of all our solemnities. In his coming down, all the feasts begin at his annunciation when he descended on the Blessed Virgin, whereby the Son of God did take our nature, the nature of man.

And in the Holy Ghost's coming they end, even in his descending this day upon the sons of men, whereby they become "partakers" of his nature, the nature of God.'[25] From the annunciation to Mary to the growth of the Church all is one action of the grace of God. The theme of deification, our being made God by grace, takes its true place at the heart of Christian teaching.

So from the sacrament of our new birth, Baptism, Andrewes goes forward, and as in all his Christmas sermons, draws his teaching to a close by applying it to the Eucharist which is about to be celebrated. Nothing demonstrates more vividly the way in which, in Andrewes's thought, theology is meant to end in worship, than these conclusions to his sermons; in them the liturgical purpose of all is revealed. What is said leads on to what is done. And here on Christmas day, the day when the Word was made flesh, it is naturally of Christ's presence with us in the body that he wishes to speak. Christ is present with us in many ways, he says; but this day

hath a special *cum* of itself, peculiar to it. Namely that we be so with him, as he this day was 'with us'; that was in the flesh, not in spirit only. That flesh that was conceived and this day born (*Corpus aptasti Mihi*) that body that was this day fitted to him. And if we be not with Him thus, if this His flesh be not "with us", if we partake it not, which way soever else we be with Him, we come short of the *Im* of this day. *Im* otherwise it may be, but not that way which is proper to this feast. 'Thy land, O Immanuel', saith the Prophet in the next chapter; and may not I say, This Thy feast, Immanuel? Sure no being with Him so kindly, so pleasing to Him, so fitting this feast, as to grow into one with Him; as upon the same day, so the very same way He did 'with us'.

This, as it is most proper, so it is the most straight and near that can be – the surest being withall that can be. *Nihil tam nobiscus, tam nostrum, quam alimentum nostrum*, 'nothing so with us, so sure, as that we eat and drink down', which goeth, and groweth one with us. For *alimentum et alitum* do *coalescere in unum*, 'grow into an union'; at that union is inseparable ever after. This then I commend to you, even the being with Him in the Sacrament of His Body – that Body that was conceived and born, as for other ends so for this specially, to be 'with you'; and this day, as for other intents, so even for this, for the

Holy Eucharist. This as the kindliest for the time, as the surest for the manner of being with.[26]

It is interesting that one of the things which Andrewes seems concerned to emphasize here is the gradual growth into union with God, symbolized and effected by eating and drinking, two of the most basic human activities by which we assimilate things not into our minds, but into our bodies, that they may be the basis for our life. Here again, he draws out strongly the relation of the incarnation to the sacraments, though we must note that he does not do so in an exclusive way. It is not only for this end, not only for this intent that Christ has taken a body, for as he asserts at the beginning, there are many ways in which he is with us. The Eucharist must not be set alone, in splendid isolation; it is the centre of a whole network of means of grace, the heart of the mystery of the Church, and it is rightly understood when it is seen in this large and inclusive context. This whole passage of Andrewes might be an exposition of the position succinctly outlined by Hooker in the words which we have already quoted, where he asks us to consider 'how God is in Christ, then how Christ is in us, and how the Sacraments do serve to make us partakers of Christ'. Hooker and Andrewes, almost exact contemporaries, employ very different styles and methods of teaching. The development of their thought, so far as we know, went on independently of each other. It was to be of momentous importance for the whole future of Anglicanism, that in their essential conclusions they should have come so close together.

Before we leave Andrewes, we must look at part of another of these eucharistic endings, perhaps the finest and most beautiful of them all. It comes at the end of the Sixteenth Sermon on the Nativity, one which has for its text the words from Ephesians: 'That in the dispensation of the fullness of times, he might gather together into one all things, both which are in Heaven, and which are in earth, even in him.' Here Andrewes expounds the incarnation as being the fulfilment and gathering together of time, all times. Clearly he is aware of the dimension of historical time, the age-old expectation of the people of Israel, from the faith of Abraham to the faith of the Blessed Virgin. On this subject of the hope of Israel he speaks in many places, and sometimes with special reference to Abraham who rejoices 'that his seed should be his Saviour, and out his roots should rise his Redeemer; all this joy should grow from the fruit of his own body',[27] in this way making a parallel with Mary whose faith and obedience likewise knows the joy and amazement of the divine which grows in her own body. But here it is the time of the natural order, the seasons, which particularly concerns him. They too have their contribution to make to the 'body' which has been prepared for the Christ.

In this theme of the recapitulation of the seasons of the year, there is an intimation of a strand of thought latent in the biblical tradition, which needs particularly to be developed and pondered at the present day. There can be no question in the Bible but that God's acts in history are specific, centring on the call and preparation of one people. But God's acts and God's concerns are also universal. The God of Abraham, Isaac and Jacob, is also the God of the whole human race, who makes his sun to rise on just and unjust alike. This is not only a perception of the New Testament. It is there already in the Old, in the covenant made with all humankind after the disaster of the flood: 'While earth remaineth, seed-time and harvest, and cold and heat, and summer and winter, and day and night shall not cease' (Gen. 8:22). It is this covenant with all humankind to which Barnabas and Paul appeal at Lystra when they are taken to be gods, and try to turn their hearers' minds to the living God 'which made heaven and earth, the sea and all things that are therein. . . He left not himself without witness, in that he did good and gave us food from heaven, and fruitful seasons, filling our hearts with good and gladness' (Acts 14:15-17). This doctrine of creation is by no means the whole of the gospel of God, but it is part of it without which the rest may become unearthed, unrelated to the whole of human experience, discarnate, a mere abstract theory.

All this Mary reminds us of. She is the one, who by her very existence tells us that the Word has become flesh, has entered into all the common processes of birth and growth. In the hymns of the Eastern Church she is specifically called 'the good earth', the one 'in whom all creation rejoices'. Andrewes does not develop this thought explicitly. It comes out more clearly in some of his successors. But it is a thought which may readily occur to us, as we examine this magnificent text, with its celebration of the coming together of heaven and earth, of time and eternity, in a moment which is made real for us in 'the highest perfection we can in this life aspire unto'.

For there we do not gather to Christ or of Christ, but we gather Christ Himself; and gathering Him we shall gather the tree and fruit and all upon it. For as there is a recapitulation of all in Heaven and earth in Christ, so there is a recapitulation of all in Christ in the holy Sacrament. You may see it clearly: there is in Christ the Word eternal for things in Heaven; there is also flesh for things on earth. Semblably, the Sacrament consisteth of a Heavenly and of a terrene part (it is Irenaeus' own words); the Heavenly – there the word too, the abstract of the other; the earthly – the element.

And in the elements, you may observe there is a fullness of the seasons of the natural year; of the corn-flour or harvest in the one, bread; of the wine-press or vintage in the other, wine. And in the heavenly, of the 'wheat-corn' whereto he compareth himself – bread, even 'the living Bread' (or 'Bread of life') 'that came down from Heaven'; the true Manna, whereof we may gather each his gomer. And again of him, the true Vine, as he calls himself – the blood of the grapes of that Vine. Both these issuing out of this day's recapitulation, both in *corpus autem aptasti mihi* of his day.'

It is as if the seasons had joined together in a universal dance, had formed themselves into a circlet or a crown for the celebration of this day.[28]

This makes in the Eucharist 'as I may say a kind of hypostatical union of the sign and the thing signified', and Andrewes cites Theodoret and Gelasius who both refer to the Eucharist to illustrate the faith that, in Christ, both humanity and divinity remain whole even though united in one. Then he takes the matter back again to argue against what he understands to be the teaching of Rome, saying that in the fullness of the sacrament both are truly present, the thing signified and the sign 'still full and whole in his own kind'. And here in the Eucharist there are indeed many gatherings into one, many benefits. 'One shall serve as the sum of all; that the very end of the sacrament is to gather again to God and his favour, if it happen, as oft it doth, we scatter and stray from him. And to gather us as close and near as *alimentum alito*, that is as near as may be. And as to gather us to God, so likewise each to other mutually; expressed lively in the symbols of many grains into one, and many grapes into the other. The Apostle is plain that we are all "one bread and one body, so many as are partakers of the one bread", so moulding us as it were into one loaf together. The gathering to God refers still to things in heaven, this other to men, to the things in earth here. All under one head by the common faith; all into one body mystical by mutual charity.'[29]

Andrewes's notion of recapitulation has broad import. While it refers to the binding into one of the whole of creation, it also speaks to the gathering of Christians into a new unity – a point Nicholas Lossky also makes in his study of Andrewes. Indeed, Lossky concludes that Andrewes is a theologian whose capacity as an interpreter between the divided Christian traditions has not been fully recognized.

> It would then, it seems to me, be right for Christians in dialogue with one another in the twentieth century to develop an interest in the work of Lancelot Andrewes, the preacher. In fact, in more than one area this theologian who lived at the heart of a period of crisis in western Christianity, anticipated in his sermons several lines of theological reflection that are developing more and more in ecumenical contexts . . . in particular, his conception of theology itself as an *élan* concerned with human beings in their entirety that reminds them of their responsibility to transfigure the universe that surrounds them.[30]

In this vision of the call to humankind in its entirety to be caught up in the divine life and to take responsibility for the whole creation, so that the whole creation may find its final transfiguration in God, the figure of Mary has a definite place. 'In the person of the Virgin, humanity, the flesh, cooperates actively in the incarnation of the Word of God.'

NOTES

1 Richard Hooker, *The Laws of Ecclesiastical Polity*, v. i. 3
2 L.S. Thornton, *Richard Hooker*, p. 119
3 Richard Hooker, *LEP* v. lvi. 9
4 Francis Paget, in Charles Gore (ed.), *Lux Mundi*, pp. 428-9

5   Lancelot Andrewes, *Ninety-Six Sermons*. Library of Anglo-Catholic Theology, vol. 1, p. 6
6   Nicholas Lossky, *Lancelot Andrewes the Preacher* (Oxford 1991), p. 32
7   Ibid., p. 47
8   Ibid., pp. 41-2
9   Lancelot Andrewes, op. cit., p. 5
10 Ibid., pp. 53-4
11 Ibid., p. 156
12 Ibid., pp. 185-6
13 Ibid., p. 192
14 Ibid., pp. 193-4
15 Nicholas Lossky, op. cit., pp. 75-6
16 Lancelot Andrewes, vol. 1, p. 191
17 Nicholas Lossky, op. cit., p. 78
18 Op. cit., p. 139
19 Ibid., pp. 139-40
20 Ibid., p. 140
21 Ibid., p. 141
22 From the poem of D. Gwenallt Jones (1899-1968), 'Gwlad ac Ynys'. ('Country and Island'), published originally in his collection *Gwreiddiau* (Llandysul 1959) and translated and quoted by H.A. Hodges in his article on the poet in *Sobornost* Series 6, no. 1, Summer 1970, pp. 25-33
23 Op. cit., p. 122
24 Ibid., pp. 150-1
25 *Ninety-Six Sermons*, LACT, vol. iii (Oxford 1841), pp. 145-5
26 Vol. i. pp. 151-2
27 Ibid., p. 130
28 Ibid., p. 281
29 Ibid., p. 282
30 Nicholas Lossky, op. cit., p. 352

3

'A Collision of Joys':
Jeremy Taylor

It is a striking fact that Nicholas Lossky should end his study of
the preaching of Lancelot Andrewes by speaking of its ecumenical
significance. This same ecumenical quality is noted as of primary
importance in a recent study of another great Anglican preacher
of the seventeenth century, Jeremy Taylor (1613-67). Taylor
was a very fluent writer who published much in the years of the
Commonwealth, during which he lived in retirement mostly in
Wales and was from time to time in prison. After the restoration of
the monarchy, he became Bishop of Down and Dromore in northern
Ireland. The most recent study of this work comes from the pen of
Archbishop Henry McAdoo (Archbishop of Dublin 1977-85).
McAdoo was for many years Anglican chairman of the Anglican-
Roman Catholic Commission and hence a man deeply involved in
our contemporary attempts to find a way through the controversies
of the sixteenth and seventeenth centuries. For this reason it is
particularly interesting to see how highly he rates the sacramental
thinking of Jeremy Taylor in this book *The Eucharistic Theology
of Jeremy Taylor Today* (1988). McAdoo feels that Taylor's largeness of mind and liberality of spirit have much to contribute to
contemporary debate. Despite great differences of style, as a
theologian Taylor has much in common with Andrewes, not
least in his recognition of the importance of mystery at the heart
of the whole theological enterprise.

Mystery in the eucharistic theology of Jeremy Taylor is not the
last refuge but the first and only starting point, 'the sacraments

are mysteries . . .' Unshakable at the heart of Taylor's teaching is the paradox that only by accepting its essential mystery can the eucharist, its meaning and purpose, be expounded and apprehended.[1]

What is said here of the eucharist clearly applies even more strongly to the mystery of the incarnation from which the sacrament springs and to which it always refers.

There seems in recent years to have been a growing recognition of the importance of Jeremy Taylor as a theologian. Apart from McAdoo's own work one might mention H. Boone Porter's *Jeremy Taylor, Liturgist* (1979), and the long and highly appreciative introduction by Thomas Carroll to his selection from Taylor's works in the series 'The Classics of Western Spirituality' (1990). By contrast in the past century it was as a writer, a master of English style, that Taylor was most studied and admired. The early nineteenth-century critics regarded Taylor as among the greatest of English writers, to be compared with Shakespeare, Milton and Bacon. Coleridge, Hazlitt, Charles Lamb all unite in his praises. This interest of the Romantics in the English seventeenth century, and especially the concern of Coleridge for seventeenth-century theology is a subject which deserves further study. Coleridge found in the writers of this period, not only an exposition of the Trinitarian doctrine, in which his mind was able to rest, but also a vision of the co-inherence of humankind and nature which was of the utmost importance for his own understanding of humanity's relation to the universe. In Taylor he found a writer whose style, for all its elaboration and amplitude, is not unrelated to the content of what he is saying, and whose extended metaphors fit into a picture of the world, in which every detail is related to the whole, and the whole is present in every detail. In this connection it must be said that the selection of passages made from Taylor by Logan Pearsall Smith, half a century ago, did something of a disservice to the writer. Pearsall Smith himself believed that Taylor's beauties as a prose writer were independent of the conscious content of his writing, indeed that 'in his best writing . . . what he really says, rather than what he thinks he is saying – his unconscious rather than his conscious utterance – is the thing which is of real interest and importance to us'. He consequently drew together a collection of beautiful passages, 'imaginative prose, full of colour and music', which very soon sate us with their richness and luxuriance. Taylor is a thinker who deserves to be taken more seriously than this: the style of his writing is not unrelated to the nature of what he is saying.

It is true that by comparison with the closely textured prose of Andrewes, with its taut, sharp rhythms and its frequent citations of Scripture and the Fathers, in approaching Taylor we are conscious of entering a different world. The pace is leisurely; the sentences, far from being brief and packed, expand and overflow. The abundance of imagery strikes us rather than the sequence of thought. This imaginative exuberance, which has been remarked on by all commentators, did not escape the notice of his contemporaries. In the sermon preached at his funeral, George Rust, his successor in the see of Dromore, remarked in a notable sentence, 'That which did most of all captivate and enravish was the gaiety and richness of his fancy; for he had much in him of that natural enthusiasm that inspires all great poets and orators; and there was a generous ferment in his blood and spirits, that set his fancy bravely a-work, and made it swell and teem, and become pregnant to such a degree of luxuriancy, as nothing but the greatness of his wit and judgement could have kept it within due bounds and measures.'[2]

The truth of this will become clear as we examine the way in which he speaks of the rôle of the Blessed Virgin in the scheme of redemption. If occasionally the elaboration of the style seems artificial, nonetheless we can often see a peculiar fitness in the choice of imagery to the subject being treated. Beneath the decoration a solid structure is to be discerned, and for all the difference of style it will become clear that the faith which is expressed is the same as that of Andrewes. There is, as we shall discover, a remarkable consistency of outlook in the members of this school.

The passages in which Taylor discusses our subject occur for the most part in the opening chapters of his Life of Christ, *The Great Exemplar:* an amply meditative retelling of parts of the gospel narrative. Here, reflection on the figure of Mary is by no means avoided. And Taylor finds much that we are to learn from her. She is, for him, first and foremost, the type of prayer and silent contemplation. As we shall see, he makes an elaborate contrast between her calling and that of St Paul. This may have been intended as a rebuke to any tendency to elevate her altogether above all other saints and to ascribe to her all virtues, by showing that she had those virtues proper to her estate. But it also enables him to develop his appreciation of the contemplative element in her life, in a way fully in harmony with the older tradition, common to East and West alike, which pictures her as specially dedicated to prayer. While he speaks in exuberant terms of the exaltation of her soul at the message of the angel, he also insists on the deep inner stillness which possessed her, in such a way as to suggest a profound understanding of the difference between the secret work of grace in the depths of the heart, and some of the more spectacular effects which at times accompany it. In speaking of the way in which joy necessarily communicates itself, he also stresses that the work of grace must at times be hidden, and is constantly progressing in ways and at times 'where no eye observes'. In all these passages there is a profound sense that grace fulfils nature, and that in Mary the good earth brings forth the fruit for which God originally made it.

When we come to examine these texts more closely we cannot do better than to begin with the paragraph where Taylor speaks of Mary's reaction at the time of the annunciation.

> When the blessed Virgin was so ascertained, that she should be a mother and a maid, and that two glories, like the two luminaries of heaven, should meet in her, that she might in such a way become the mother of her Lord, that she might with better advantages be his servant; then all her hopes and her desires received such satisfaction, and filled all the corners of her heart so much, as indeed it was fain to make room for its reception. But she to whom the greatest things of religion, and the transportations of devotion, were made familiar, by the assiduity and piety of her daily practices, however she was full of joy, yet she was carried like a full vessel, without the violent tossings of a tempestuous passion, or the wrecks of a stormy imagination: and as the power of the Holy Ghost did descend upon her like rain into a fleece of wool, without any obstreperous noises or violences to nature, but only the extraordinariness of an exaltation, so her spirit received it with the gentleness and tranquillity fitted for the entertainment of the spirit of love, and a quietness symbolical to the holy guest of her spotless womb, the Lamb of God . . .[3]

We start here with the familiar theme of the conjunction of opposites, motherhood and virginity, and with the thought of the fulfilment of hopes and aspirations. But we pass almost immediately to the striking image of the ship in full cargo, carried forward by the strength of the gale, but not thrown about like a ship without ballast. It is an image which demands consideration. There is a recognition here of the many levels of human response to the divine activity, which while it may touch the surface and cause apparent disturbance, yet is most truly known in the depths of the human spirit, in certain hidden and basic orientations of will and desire which express themselves in the constancy of daily practice. There is a joy which is strong, which impels us forward like a great gale of wind, but which is yet silent and secure and does not disperse or agitate the human spirit. Here is a theme which Taylor underlines, the depth, the constancy of her prayer, that continual turning towards the mystery of God in faith and expectation. 'There are some curiosities so bold and determinate, as to tell the very matter of her prayer', at the moment of the annunciation 'and that she was praying for the salvation of all the world, and the revelation of the Messias. . . We have no security of the particular; but there is no piety so diffident as to require a sign to create belief that her employment at the instant was holy and religious . . .'4 It is a typically Anglican statement, refraining from too confident a speculation, yet not refusing the substance behind the over-creative imagination of earlier writers.

This conviction about the hidden, silent centre of Mary's life finds full expression in the passage where Taylor makes his comparison between the Blessed Virgin and St Paul.

> And it is not altogether inconsiderable to observe, that the holy Virgin came to a great perfection and state of piety by a few, and those modest and even external actions. St Paul travelled over the world, preached to the Gentiles, disputed against the Jews, confounded heretics, writ excellently learned letters, suffered dangers, injuries, affronts and persecutions to the height of wonder, and by these violences of life, action and patience, obtained the crown of an excellent religion and devotion. But the holy Virgin, although she engaged sometimes in an active life, and in the exercises of an ordinary and small economy

and government, or ministries of a family, yet she arrived to
her perfections by the means of a quiet and silent piety, the
internal actions of love, devotion, and contemplation; and
instructs us, that not only those who have opportunity and powers
of a magnificent religion, or a pompous charity, or miraculous
conversion of souls, or assiduous and effectual preachings, or
exterior demonstrations of corporal mercy, shall have the greatest
crown, and the addition of degrees and accidental rewards; but
the silent reflections, the splendours of an internal devotion, the
unions of love, humility and obedience, the daily offices of prayer
and praises sung to God, the acts of faith and fear, of patience and
meekness, of hope and reverence, repentance and charity,
and those graces which walk in a veil and silence, make
great ascents to God, and as sure progress to favours and a
crown, as the more ostentatious and laborious exercises of a
more solemn religion. No man needs to complain of a want
of power or opportunities for religious perfections; a devout
woman in her closet, praying with much zeal and affection for
the conversion of souls, is in the same order to a 'shining like
stars in glory' as he who by excellent discourses puts it into a
more forward disposition to be actually performed. And possibly
her prayers obtained energy and force to my sermon, and made
the ground fruitful, and the seed spring up to life eternal.[5]

The passage is, on many levels, not unworthy of its author.
Even by Taylor's standards the third sentence of the paragraph must
be allowed to be ample. But behind the luxuriance of the rhetoric
there is personal experience at work. At the end we suddenly
become aware of the extent to which the whole comparison has
been moulded by Taylor's own experience of his relationship with
the devout ladies, particularly Lady Anne Carbery, who helped him
during the period of the Commonwealth. We may wonder too how
much this reflection on the reality and meaning of an inner life,
withdrawn from external and spectacular activity, was stimulated
by his own enforced retirement throughout the period of the Puritan
ascendancy. The experience of persecution can have the effect of
deepening and strengthening convictions which had formerly been
theoretical. This seems to have been the case with Taylor. He was
a man who had made many inner discoveries.

Towards the end of the 1650s when he was living in Northern Ireland, he could write to a friend of 'the experimental secret way' of progress and religion.

> My retirement in this solitary place hath been, I hope, of some advantage to me as to this state of religion, in which I am yet but a novice. . . I beg of you to assist me with your prayers, and to obtain of God for me that I may arrive at that height of love and union with God which is given to all those souls who are very dear to God.[6]

We sense something of the same quality in the notable sermon which Taylor preached at Trinity College Dublin in the following decade on the relation between life and doctrine. The whole sermon is an urgent plea for the putting aside of angry polemic and controversy, for a willingness to listen and understand, for a recognition that doctrine is to issue in life and to issue from life.

> The way to judge of religion is by doing of our duty; and theology is rather a divine life than a divine knowledge. In heaven indeed we shall first see and then love; but here on earth we must first love, and love will open our eyes as well as our hearts and we shall then see and then perceive and understand.[7]

A little further on in the sermon Taylor again hints at the direct knowledge of divine things which the way of prayer may open up.

> Lastly, there is a sort of God's dear servants who walk in perfectness, who 'perfect holiness in the fear of God'; and they have a degree of clarity and divine knowledge, more than we can discourse of, and more certain than the demonstrations of geometry, brighter than the sun, and indeficient as the light of heaven. This is called by the Apostle the απαύγασμα του Θεού. Christ is the brightness of God, manifested in the hearts of his dearest servants. But I shall say no more of this at this time, for this is to be felt and not to be talked of, and they that never touched it with their finger, may secretly perhaps laugh at it in

their heart, and be never the wiser. All that I shall now say of it is this, that a good man is united unto God as a flame touches a flame and combines unto splendour and to glory; so is the spirit of man united unto Christ by the Spirit of God.[8]

Behind and through such hints and affirmations we can perceive something of great significance, a sense of the human calling to union with God; a profound conviction about the meaning of a life wholly given to the inner work of prayer; some intuition, some glimpse of the meaning of the contemplative life, still vividly present in the seventeenth century, despite the absence of monastic communities. It gives us an insight into the quality of seventeenth-century religion and the depth of prayer which lies behind Taylor's liturgical interests and projects. Human life can expand and unfold, can grow and mature towards God inwardly as well as outwardly. There is an inner journey, as well as an outer one, with its own dangers and temptations. 'Those graces which walk in a veil and silence' – the phrase is one which justifies Taylor's older reputation as a stylist – 'make great ascents to God'.

But this is not the only phrase of an exceptional beauty to be found in this section of Taylor's work. Another occurs in the passage where he is meditating on the fact that Mary had apparently not told Joseph of the message of the angel. 'It is in some circumstances and from some persons more secure to conceal visions and those heavenly gifts, which create estimates among men, than to publish them, which may possibly minister to vanity; and those exterior graces may do God's work, though no observer note them, but the person for whose sake they are sent: like rain falling in uninhabited valleys, where no eye observes the showers; yet the valleys laugh and sing to God in their refreshment without a witness.'[9] How powerfully the picture of rain falling in lonely upland valleys where no eye observes it, suggests the continued, silent generosity of the divine activity, always at work throughout the whole creation, effective in ways we neither know nor understand, causing the earth to laugh and sing to God its creator. The image itself puts before us the idea of the Blessed Virgin as the type of the receptivity and fruitfulness of the order of nature, springing up in response to the initiative of God. It is an idea which constantly recurs when men and women begin to meditate on her calling.

However, it is not only the secret work of God which Taylor celebrates in his meditation on the life of the Virgin as it is portrayed by St Luke. There is also the visitation to consider. 'And she, who was now full of God, bearing God in her virgin womb, and the Holy Spirit in her heart, who had also overshadowed her, enabling her to a supernatural and miraculous conception, arose with haste and gladness to communicate that joy which was designed for the world. . . And Mary arose in those days and went into the hill country with haste, into a city of Judah.'[10] If there are circumstances which indicate that we should hide the gifts which are given us, and conceal our joys, nevertheless of itself joy is something to be shared, something which communicates itself to all with whom we enter into contact. Taylor does not hesitate to use all the resources of his eloquence at its most flamboyant in his attempt to communicate the exaltation and amazement of this meeting of Mary with Elizabeth.

> But the joys that the Virgin Mother had, were such as concerned all the world; and that part of them which was her peculiar, she would not conceal from persons apt to their entertainment, but go publish God's mercy towards her to another holy person, that they might join in the praises of God; as knowing that it may be convenient to represent our personal necessities in private, yet God's gracious returns and the blessings he makes to descend on us, are more fit, when there is no personal danger collaterally appendant, to be published in the communion of saints; that the hopes of others may receive increase, that their faith may grow up to become excellent and great, and the praises of God may be sung aloud, till the sound strike at heaven, and join with the hallelujahs, which the morning stars in their orbs pay to their great Creator.[11]

Human rejoicing, when it is redoubled in being shared, acquires a dimension of cosmic celebration.

> It is not easy to imagine what a collision of joys was at this blessed meeting: two mothers of two great princes, the one the greatest that was born of woman, and the other was his Lord, and these made mothers by two miracles, met together with joy and mysteriousness; where the mother of our Lord went

to visit the mother of his servant, and the Holy Ghost made the meeting a festival, and descended upon Elizabeth, and she prophesied. Never but in heaven was there more joy and ecstasy. The persons . . . meeting together to compare and unite their joys and their eucharist, and then made prophetical and inspired, must needs have discoursed like seraphim and the most ecstasied order of intelligences; for all the faculties of nature were turned into grace, and expressed in their way the excellent solemnity. 'For it came to pass when Elizabeth heard the salutation of Mary, the babe leaped in her womb; and Elizabeth was filled with the Holy Ghost.'[12]

This comparison with the orders of angels is one which we have already met in Andrewes. Here it is expressed with the extravagance of a baroque rhetoric, but for all that it is no less serious. It has its basis in those passages in the Bible which speak of humanity being created but little lower than the angels, in order to be crowned with glory and honour, and again in the words of St Paul when he declared that Christ took on him the seed of Abraham, and not the nature of angels. These are all passages which are intended to express the heights to which human nature is called, its true capacity, as revealed in the mystery of the incarnation. The faith which they embody was carried on into the tradition of the Church, and became a staple element in the hymns of the liturgy. Even if we find it difficult to accept all the traditional picture of the angelic realm, the comparison need not be without meaning for us. Principalities and powers, of one kind or another, are very familiar to us. Forces, whether personal or impersonal, which for good or evil, seem infinitely stronger and more permanent than humanity in its frailty and transience, these we know well. The message of the gospel is that over all these our personal life is triumphant, for God is within us, has united us with himself, has proved victorious over every power. The meeting of two pregnant women in an obscure Palestinian village is of greater significance than all these forces. Human life, even in its most ordinary and routine aspects has a hidden wealth of possibilities which is infinite with God's infinity.

But it is not only this point which is so striking in the two passages which have been quoted here. What cannot escape the reader is the consistently liturgical character of the thought and terminology. The liturgy is not only a meeting of humanity with God, it is also a meeting of human persons with one another, a *synaxis*, a coming together into one place. Joy and thanksgiving are things to be shared, which grow by being shared, and when this happens something which involves the whole universe begins to take place. The united praise and thanksgiving of men and women, their common prayer, rises up in unity with the praises of all creation. In this sense the meeting of Mary and Elizabeth is a beginning of Christian liturgy, and the words which the Evangelist has given to them in this moment have remained a constant part of the Church's worship. Taylor was not at all unaware of the Eastern Church's teaching about the rôle of the Holy Spirit in the Church's sacraments; like many of the Anglicans of his period he was much influenced by his study of the Eastern liturgies. So he can write of the original moment, 'the Holy Ghost made the meeting festival'. In the power of the Holy Spirit, our coming together to praise God is transformed into a coming together of humanity with God in the festival of the Kingdom; the Eucharist of the Church provides the vehicle by which our human life is lifted up into the life and energy of God. So, too, Taylor can speak at this point of the 'excellent solemnity', a term which suggests the formula of the Latin rite, which frequently speaks of the Church's festivals as 'joyful solemnities', as if to join together reminiscences of both Eastern and Western liturgical tradition.[13]

In the very phrase the 'excellent' or 'joyful solemnity', we have a junction of apparent opposites which is strange to our society, but which was more natural in a society in which festival was, though contested, still widely understood. Perhaps it was because the Church's traditional festivals, with their mixture of Christian and pre-Christian, religious and social, human and divine were so much threatened at this time, that the Anglicans had so sharp a sense of the richness of their meaning. To Taylor it is clear that a solemnity is something weighty, serious, ordered and ceremonious. It is also something ecstatic, jubilant, joyful and liberating. These things are only apparent contradictions. In fact they are complementary. Human life, both personal and social, cannot become truly human unless it contains both elements, unless it is able to unite joy and sorrow, gravity and lightness in a single complex unity of love. Throughout this passage there is an evident awareness of festival and solemnity, and an experience of a joy which is truth telling and truth revealing; of the mingling of human and divine which is one of the characteristic notes of Christian worship, and which derives from the union of the two natures, human and divine, in Christ, which is the heart of its message of goodness. 'For all the faculties of nature were turned into grace, and expressed in their way the excellent solemnity.' The many different faculties of humankind, feeling, willing, thinking, acting are brought together into one, integrated and made whole when the Holy Spirit touches the human spirit in the act of worship. All our being from the root up, from the very 'groundsill' as Andrewes says, is liberated into the kingdom of God's grace.

Taylor, of course, thinks of this meeting of Mary and Elizabeth as unique. He speaks of 'two mothers of two great princes'. But he knows that these princes are so only in a hidden, paradoxical way. And though indeed on any Christian reckoning this meeting was unique, yet it is implied that it was also universal. The meeting of any two people when the Holy Spirit makes 'the meeting festival', may be filled with 'joy and mysteriousness'. The meeting of two women carrying in their bodies, as well as in their hope and love, the promises of two new, unknown lives may be doubly so. We learn something here not only about the nature of liturgical celebration, but also of personal relationship. Again the hidden potential of humanity is revealed.

Both thoughts are present in the words with which Taylor introduces his meditation on the Magnificat.

The blessed Virgin Mary hearing her cousin full of spirit and prophecy, calling her blessed, and praising her faith, and confirming her joy, instantly sang her hymn to God, returning those praises, which she received, to him to whom they did appertain. For so we should worship God with all our praises, being willing upon no other condition to extend our hand to receive our own honour, but that with the other we might transmit it to God; that as God is honoured in all his creatures, so he may be honoured in us too; looking upon the graces which God hath given us, but as greater instruments and abilities to serve him, being none of ours, but talents which are intrusted into our banks to be improved.[14]

The thought is a profound one. The circulation of divine life, which comes out from God into the creation, returns to God enriched with the gratitude of humanity, having received a human form. In hidden, unknown ways, no less than in the public thanksgiving, the Eucharist of the Christian assembly, God's glory is made known and the creation itself is glorified in him.

In his meditation on the theme of Mary as mother, it appears more than once that Taylor is anxious to avoid any tendency to disparage marriage in comparison with virginity. Both estates are good, both to be honoured. He himself was married twice, and in his writings as a whole we can find a certain fluctuation of view, at times an exaltation of virginity, as for instance in *Holy Living*, where in some sections he envisages the situation of 'virgins that offer that state to God, and mean not to enter into the state of marriage', and at times an exaltation of married life. Here he attempts to keep a balance.

> When the eternal God meant to stoop so low as to be fixed to our centre, he chose for his mother a holy person and a maid, yet affianced to a just man, that he might not only be secured in the innocency, but also provided for in the reputation of his mother . . .
>
> And yet her marriage was more mysterious; for as, besides the miracle it was an eternal honour and advancement to the glory of virginity, that he chose a virgin for his mother, so it was in that manner attempered, that the Virgin was betrothed, lest honourable marriage might be disrupted, and seem inglorious, by a positive rejection from any participation of the honour . . .[15]

It is this concern for the honour of marriage and for the meaning of maternity, which seems to lie behind the *First Discourse*, or excursus, which punctuates *The Great Exemplar*, and which has as its subject, 'Of nursing children'. An earlier generation than our own, which had not known the work of Freud and Klein, might have been surprised at the amount of space which Taylor gives to this discussion of the importance of breastfeeding, and of the value of the mother herself nursing her child. Taylor still lives in a world which can take the psychosomatic unity of human nature as a given and commonly understood reality. We live in a time which is seeking to recover this insight. For him it is clear that our higher, more spiritual acts and virtues are all rooted in our most basic bodily needs and instincts. The virtues, the distinctively human qualities and actions all grow from this physical basis which humankind shares with the animals. The question of feeding infants may seem at first sight a trivial one, but in so far as it is through its relationship with its mother that the child's capacity for relationship with other people and with the outside world is first exercised and developed, it is not trivial at all.

> Although other actions are more perfect and spiritual, yet this is more natural and humane; other things being superadded to a full duty, rise higher, but this builds stronger, and is like a part of the foundation, having no lustre, but much strength; and however the others are full of ornament, yet this hath in it some degree of necessity, and possibly is with more danger and irregularity omitted, than actions, which spread their leaves fairer, and look more gloriously.[16]

If the foundations are not well laid the whole subsequent work of building will suffer.

It is not surprising that there is no other section of the Life of Christ in which Taylor reflects at such length on the place of Mary, as in these opening chapters. But he cannot omit to speak of her when he comes to meditate on the crucifixion. Nor does his eloquence desert him here. But what is more striking is the degree in which he is faithful to his first conviction about her. Just as the joys of the annunciation were not enough to overthrow her inner silence of spirit, so even the grief of the crucifixion, the sword which goes through her own heart, meets in her heart a greater reality of calm and steadfast love.

> By the cross of Christ stood the holy Virgin-mother, upon whom old Simeon's prophecy was now verified; for now she felt 'a sword piercing through her very soul'; she stood without clamour and womanish noises; sad, silent, and with a modest grief, deep as the waters of the abyss, but smooth as the face of a pool; full of love, and patience, and sorrow and hope. Now she

was put to it to make use of all those excellent discourses her holy Son had used to build up her spirit, and fortify it against this day. Now she felt the blessings and strengths of faith; and she passed from the griefs of the passion to the expectation of the resurrection; and she rested in this death, as in a sad remedy; for she knew it reconciled God with all the world. But her hope drew a veil before her sorrow; and though her grief was great enough to swallow her up, yet her love was greater, and did swallow up her grief.[17]

Such lines can, of course, give us no historical information about the attitude of the Blessed Virgin at this moment. The sceptical exegete will rightly remind us that the gospel tells us directly nothing whatsoever about it, though the narrative in the Fourth Gospel is eloquent enough, for all its economy. But as we read them, we may well think of countless representations of the crucifixion in which the mother of the crucified man is depicted as calm and upright, in contrast with the distraught grief of the other onlookers. These are things which represent profound convictions about the nature of grief; that the truest and strongest thoughts and feelings are often ones which lie too deep for outward expression whether in word or gesture; that a great calm need not be a sign either of indifference or insensibility; but that in those whose lives have been hidden in God in constant prayer, such calm may be a reflection of an inner stability based in the constant love of God himself, 'deep as the waters of the abyss, but smooth as the face of a pool'. We are reminded of Taylor's earlier words about the serenity of the mother in the moment of her greatest joy. Here is a similar intuition, which may well lead us to a reticence like that of the gospel narratives.

NOTES

1   H.R. McAdoo, *The Eucharistic Theology of Jeremy Taylor Today* (Norwich 1988), p. 203
2   *The Whole Works of the Rt. Revd. Jeremy Taylor* (1835), vol. i, p. lxx
3   Ibid., p. 28
4   Ibid., p. 29
5   Ibid., pp. 29-30

6 Quoted in Margaret Cropper, *Flame Touches Flame* (1949), p. 143
7 Jeremy Taylor, *Selected Works*, ed. T.K. Carroll (New York 1990), p. 361
8 Ibid., pp. 375-6
9 Op. cit., p. 32
10 Ibid., p. 30
11 Ibid., p. 31
12 Ibid., p. 31
13 For an excellent study of Taylor's work as a liturgist see H. Boone Porter, *Jeremy Taylor, Liturgist* (1978). Dr Porter stresses the way in which Taylor brings together Eastern and Western influences in his liturgical work.
14 Op. cit., p. 32
15 Ibid., p. 29
16 Ibid., p. 38
17 Ibid., p. 340

4

'The Virgin Mother, the Eternal Son':
Mark Frank and Herbert Thorndike

If neither Andrewes nor Taylor is widely read at present, their names at least are fairly familiar. This is not the case with Mark Frank, who on any ordinary reckoning would have to be judged one of the secondary figures of this period. Dying in 1664, at the age of fifty-one, Frank did not have time to reach the eminence which would surely have been his, had he lived longer. Fellow of Pembroke College, Cambridge, and after the restoration of the monarchy Master of the College, Frank reveals himself in his sermons a true disciple in the school of Lancelot Andrewes. In his preaching the balanced theology of this period of Anglican divinity, nourished on Scripture and the Fathers alike, finds eloquent expression. Indeed of all the Anglican preachers of this time he speaks most fully about Mary; and we are not surprised to find in him a powerful sense of the meaning of the liturgy, and of the place of the human body in his approach to God. It is some measure of the richness of the seventeenth century that we can find writing of such quality in one who is so little known.

There is in Frank's sermons, at times, a sharp polemical note, occasioned by the controversies with the Puritans. When we reflect that some of the sermons which we have, must have been preached during the Commonwealth, in private, semi-clandestine assemblies, at a time when Frank was deprived of his fellowship, this is hardly surprising. What is more striking is the generally serene way in which he expounds his teaching and seeks to find a *via media* between the clashing opinions of his contemporaries. We can hear in him an outstanding spokesman of that older way of seeing things, which was soon to collapse under the impact of the philosophy of Descartes and the first beginnings of scientific inquiry. He still thinks with confidence of a human being as a microcosm placed at the centre of a universe where all is inter-related. He can still employ that highly metaphysical style which sees a detailed correspondence between the inner and outer worlds. It is interesting to speculate whether, had he lived another twenty years, he could have continued to preach in this same style, and with the same emphasis.

Since Frank's sermons are virtually unknown, and since he is a preacher who needs to be quoted at length we shall not hesitate to make lengthy quotations from them, gradually becoming familiar with his theological method and approach, before we come to see what he has to say specifically on the subject of Mary. His exposition of the place of Mary in the scheme of redemption needs to be seen in context if it is to be evaluated properly. The theme of joy in God, and its proper expression, which we have already seen in Andrewes and in Taylor, is one which finds eloquent expression in his work. It is a subject which demands our attention in this connection. So in a sermon for Easter we read

> . . .the joy that God requires in the things that he has made, or any time makes for us, is not only inward, it must issue out into outward acts; out into the mouth to sing forth his praise, 'in psalms and hymns and spiritual songs'; out into the feet to go up to the house of God with the posture as well as the voice of joy and gladness, to go up with haste, to worship with reverence, to stand up cheerfully at the hymns and songs of praise; our very bones, as David speaks, to rejoice too; the very clattered bones to clatter together and rejoice; all the parts and powers of the body to make some expression in their way and order.[1]

Joy, as Frank constantly teaches, is something which makes us grow, which makes for an expansion of the human heart and mind, an expansion which is to find personal and inward expression, and also to have social and ethical consequences. It is very striking in the passage below, that the social and economic dimensions of human life are involved, no less than those which we are apt to call strictly religious. Speaking of the 'exceeding joy' which the Wise Men knew when they found the way to Bethlehem, he says in an Epiphany sermon,

Being so exceeding, it will exceed also the narrow compass of the inward man, will issue out also into the outward, into the tongue and head. Joy is the dilatation, the opening of the heart, and sending out the spirits into all the parts. And if this joy we have, it will open our hearts to praise him; open our hearts to heaven to receive its influence; open our hearts to our needy brother, to compassionate and relieve him; it will send out life, and heat, and spirit into all our powers – into our lips, to sing unto him, into our fingers, to play to him, into our feet, even to leap for joy; into our eyes, perpetually to gaze upon him; into our hands, to open them for his sake plentifully to the poor; into the whole body, to devote it wholly to his service. This is the wise men's joy, 'great' and 'exceeding'.[2]

Generosity to those who need, inward exaltation of spirit, outward participation in the Christian assembly, all these things go together, when God breathes his own life into the dry, scattered bones of our existence and raises us up into true humanity, drawing together body and soul in a unity of adoration, and opening our life alike to heaven and to our neighbour.

But not the powers of the body alone, but all the powers of the soul too: 'Praise the Lord, O my soul, and all that is within me praise his holy name'. Our souls magnify the Lord, our spirits rejoice in God our Saviour; our memories recollect and call to mind his benefits and what he has done for us; our hearts evaporate into holy flames and ardent affections and desires after him; our wills henceforward to give up themselves wholly to him as their only hope and joy. It is no perfect joy where any of them is wanting. It is but dissembled joy where all is outward. It is but imperfect gladness where all is within. It must be both. God this day raised the body, the body therefore must raise itself, and rise up to praise him. He this day gave us hope he would not leave our souls in hell; fit, therefore, it is the soul should leave all to praise him that sits in heaven. He is not worthy of the day or the benefit of the day, worthy to be raised again, who will not this day rise to praise; not worthy to rise at the resurrection of the just who will not rise today in the congregation of the righteous to testify his joy and gladness in the resurrection of his Saviour and his own.[3]

The fullness of joy then involves the integration of all human faculties. The theme which we have found in Jeremy Taylor is found again here. This joy leads men and women out beyond themselves into the very life of God. The great insistence on the participation of the body in this life is particularly significant. We need to see it in a large historical perspective. As Aelred Squire remarks, 'Particularly in the West one of the unobserved consequences of the Schism with the East was that, with the development of the scholastic movement, a schism between flesh and spirit was gradually established both in theory and practice. Reinforced by the philosophy of Descartes, and accentuated by the social results of the Industrial Revolution, this cleavage between the bodily and the spiritual has left us in our own period with a Christianity unbelievably discarnate.'[4]

This is the version of Christianity against which many of our contemporaries have revolted, most notably those concerned with ecology and with the rediscovery of the place of humankind in the material world. Many indeed have supposed that this 'unbelievably discarnate' form of religion is itself Christianity. No one can deny its influence in the West particularly in the Puritan movement and in those forms of Protestantism which have minimized the importance of the sacraments and distrusted the whole realm of the symbolical. But Frank stands for an older and wider tradition of classical Christian faith and understanding. This is a tradition rooted in the Bible no less than in the life of the early Christian centuries. Here it is understood that humankind in its totality is redeemed; that we can offer the whole of our life, body no less than soul and spirit to the service of God. This vision is central in the work of the seventeenth-century Anglicans. It lies behind their concern for the details of ceremonial in worship, a concern which has seemed to some commentators fussy and unbalanced. As Nicholas Ferrar insisted in one of his last conversations with his brother John, 'It is the right, good old way you are in; keep in it. God will be worshipped in spirit and truth, in soul and in body. He will have both inward love and fear, and outward reverence of body and gesture.'[5]

This same concern lies behind their insistence on the keeping of the Church's festivals and in the celebration of the feasts of the Church, which thus become anticipations, foretastes of the feast of the Kingdom, that celebration of life and joy for which the world was made in the beginning, to which it will be drawn in the end of all things. In the feasts, and above all in the Eucharist, eternity enters into time, and time is taken up into eternity.

Again, it may be that the abolition of the festivals under the Commonwealth contributed to the particularly vivid perception which Frank has of their significance. Certainly he has a wonderful perception of the meaning of liturgical time. He gives us one of the few seventeenth-century Anglican sermons on the transfiguration, and dwells with pleasure on the origin of the name 'Candlemas', the Feast of the Presentation. The very multiplicity of the festivals is full of meaning to him. They seek, in time, to reveal something of the richness and the generosity of the divine being and the divine action. They also succeed in drawing together all the diversities of the human race. They are all occasions of blessing.

> For this day also of his presentation, as well as those others of his birth, circumcision and manifestation – Candlemas-day as well as Christmas-day, New Year's day, or Epiphany, is a day of blessing; a day of God's blessing us, and our blessing of him again; of Christ's being presented for us, and our presenting to him again; of his presenting in the temple, and our presenting ourselves in the Church, to bless God and him for his presentation, his presentation-day and our Candlemas, our little candles, our petty lights, our souls reflecting back to this great light, that was this day presented in the temple and then darted down upon us.
>
> The shepherds blessed God in the morn of his nativity; the wise men upon Epiphany; Simeon and Anna, today. All conditions before, all sexes today; ignorant shepherds and learned clerks, poor countrymen and great princes, no condition out before, and both sexes in today. Sinners both of Jew and Gentile, men that most stood in need of a Saviour, before; just and righteous souls today; that we might know there is none so good but stands in need of him one day or other – that will want a Saviour, if not at Christmas, yet at Candlemas; if not among

sinners, yet among the righteous, either first or last. Mary the blessed, Joseph the just, Simeon the devout, Anna the religious, all in today, as at the end of Christmas; like the chorus to the angel's choir, to bear a part in the angels' anthem, to make up a full choir of voices to glorify God for this great present, which brings peace to the earth, and good-will among men.[6]

We cannot but be struck, in this passage, by the preacher's appreciation of the significance of this whole cycle of the feasts of Christmas, all of which are feasts of the incarnation. All of them necessarily involve our Lady and in all of them we ourselves are involved with her. Frank's use of the vernacular names for the feasts is also significant. It suggests a regard for the popular traditions surrounding them, and links with the thought that people of all conditions are to be drawn together, into the festival of faith. The Church in its worship is inclusive and catholic. There is nothing narrow or sectarian about it.

This point is made again in the first of his Advent sermons, where Frank quotes St John Chrysostom on the monastic life, in order to stress that all, secular and religious alike, are called to take their part in the univeral act of thanksgiving. 'Nor were these multitudes choirs of priests and clerks, or only orders of religious men; it was a congregation of seculars, though there were priests and Apostles in it. It is St Chrysostom's own note, to tell us, men are not to put off the work of devotion and religion wholly to the priest and clerk, as if they only were to sing the Benedictus, Hosannas or Alleluiahs, and the multitudes only stand looking on; or think men in some religious orders were only obliged to live orderly and like Christians, all secular or laymen as they pleased. *Non ita sane, non ita est*, says he, "It is not so indeed, it is not so."'[7] This is a passage of interest not only in that it tells us that people of all kinds are to take their share in the Church's celebration, but also because it seems to assume that the Church will include as well as laymen, priests and clerks, 'men in some religious orders', 'orders of religious men', an assumption not very common among seventeenth-century Anglicans. But all are to unite in the celebration of God's gift; and all the feasts of the year make present different aspects of this one reality. The gift of eternity is made now in the liturgy of the Church. We may suspect that when Frank speaks of glorifying God 'for this great present', there is a double meaning, either consciously or unconsciously there.

It is in the mystery of the Eucharist, that this presence is above all made known. Here the reality of the incarnation is made present with us. Like Andrewes, Frank never isolates the coming of Christ in the sacrament from his other ways of coming to us, but he does not hesitate to place this mystery at the centre.

> And there is a visit he is now coming today to make us, as much to be wondered at as any – that he should feed us with his body, and yet that be in heaven; and that he should cheer us with his blood, and yet that shed so long ago; that he should set his throne and keep his table and presence upon the earth, and yet heaven his throne and earth his footstool; that he should here pose all our understandings with his mysterious work, and so many ages of Christians, after so many years of study and assistance of the Spirit, not yet be able to understand it. 'What is man' or 'the son of man', O blessed Jesu, that thou shouldst thus also visit and confound him with the wonders of thy mercy and goodness?
>
> Here also is glory and honour too, to be admitted to his table; nowhere so great; to be made one with Him, as the meat is with the body; no glory like it. Here is the crown of plenty: fullness of pardon, grace, and heavenly benediction. Here is the crown of glory; nothing but rays and beauties, lustres and glories, to be seen in Christ, and darted from him into pious souls. Come take your crowns, come compass your-selves with those eternal circlings.
>
> Take now the 'cup of salvation', and remember God for so remembering you: call upon the name of the Lord, and give glory to your God. If you cannot speak out fully (as who can speak, in such amazements as these thoughts may seriously work in us?) cast yourselves down in silence, and utter out your souls in these or the like broken speeches: What is man, Lord, what is man? . . . What shall I say? How shall I sufficient admire?[8]

Here again we find the tone of serious ecstasy which we have discovered in Andrewes. The mind falls silent before the mystery, which so many centuries of study and reflection have not been able to fathom. In the Eucharist the fullness of God's love is made present before us, the greatness of our human calling is revealed.

We recognize the coming together in one of heaven and earth, past and present, God and humankind; they are gathered together in a circle, a crown, an emblem of eternity. Human life is crowned, finds its fulfilment in the eternity for which we are made in the beginning. 'Let us crown his altars then with offerings, and his name with praise; let us be often *in corona*, in the congregation of them that praise him, among such as keep holiday. Let us crown his courts with beauty, crown ourselves with good works; they should be our glory and our crown: and for the worship that he crowns us with too, let us worship and give him honour, so remember, so visit, so crown him again . . .'9

One of the salient facts that we know about Mark Frank's life is his close association as a young man with the family at Little Gidding. He seems to have been a particularly close friend of Nicholas Ferrar junior, the nephew of the elder Nicholas Ferrar who was the spiritual director of the whole enterprise. It was Mark Frank who composed the epitaph for the brilliant young man. It is not altogether surprising that we do not find any direct references to the family of Little Gidding in the sermons of Mark Frank. But knowing, as we do, of his connection with them, we can hardly fail to find traces of the influence of their life in his preaching. There is his evident feeling for such monastic practices as fasting and watching, his sense that the Church includes people in religious orders, his sense of the reality of prayer and the full dimensions of joy; all things which he would have seen in practice in the life of the Ferrars, and some of them things not widely appreciated among seventeenth-century Anglicans. There is a certain air of light and beauty in all the descriptions of their common life at Little Gidding which finds expression in these sermons too.

It is reported of St Lucian the Martyr, that he converted many by his modest, cheerful and pious look and carriage; and of St Bernard, that, *In carne ejus apparebat gratia quaedam spiritualis*, etc., 'There appeared a kind of spiritual grace throughout his body'; there shone a heavenly brightness in his face; there darted an angelical purity and dove-like simplicity from his eyes; so great was the inward beauty of his inward man, that it poured out itself in his whole outward man abundantly over all his parts and powers; no motion in them but reason and religion. Where such

virtue is, it will be 'known', must be too: must be so expressed
that men may know and feel the benefits and effects.[10]

We feel ourselves, in such a passage, to be in contact with a
man who has some direct knowledge of what he is speaking about,
who himself has seen men and women who have impressed him in
this way. This impression becomes all the stronger in a remark
which occurs in the sermon for St Stephen's Day. 'Sometimes it is
(oftener it has been when the beginning of Christianity needed it at
first), that by some visible comforts and discoveries he shows himself
to the dying saint. Often it is that the soul ready to depart feels
some sensible joys and ravishments to uphold its ailing spirits.'[11]
The story of Nicholas Ferrar's deathbed, his sudden raising up
of himself at the very moment when he was accustomed to rise
for prayer, his exclamation, 'I have been at a feast . . . at the
feast of the great King', his sudden passing – all these things
must have been familiar to Mark Frank, and they can hardly
have been absent from his mind when he wrote these words.

So the order and the beauty of the life which he saw at
Little Gidding entered deeply into his heart and mind. On the
subject of order he writes at the beginning of a sermon for St
Peter's Day, 'I begin with St Peter's ill success, and that is no
comfortable beginning; but it is the beginning of the text, and
I love order everywhere, though it cost never so dear to keep
that.'[12] We are not surprised to find an Anglican of his period
emphatic on the necessity of order. But on the subject of beauty
he has yet finer things to say. 'Christ's beauty is God's blessing;
all beauty is so, be it what it will; from him it comes, is but
a ray of that eternal beauty, that inaccessible light, that *summe
pulchrum* as well as *summe bonum*, the everlasting brightness of
the Father; all the beauty of the mind and body, all the integrity
and vigour of all our powers, are merely from his blessing, not our
merit – a good lesson from it, not to be proud of any of them.'[13]

This restoration of the integrity and vigour of the powers of
humanity is a thing which has consequences for all creation; for the
praise of God which rises up from all things is to become vocal and
articulate through humankind. In the psalms of David all things are
said to praise God, and in a strange passage Frank enumerates them
all, one by one. Then he continues, 'Yet how should all these

things we mentioned do it? Many of them have no tongue to say, many no sense to understand it. Why, they do it yet.' All things can praise God in and through humankind, the priest of nature. So in this Christmas sermon, the preacher goes on,

> The sun by day, the moon by night, may become torches to light his servants' service. The earth brings forth her corn and wine to furnish out his table; the deep gives up her riches, and brings home golds and silks to adorn his holy altars; the earth brings stones and minerals, the hills and mountains trees and cedars to his house; the fire kindles tapers for it; all the meteors of the air, and all the seasons of the years, do somewhat; every wind blows somewhat towards it. The very birds and swallows get as near the altar as they can to bless him; the snow and cold and ice crowd as near Christmas as they can, to bear a part in this great solemnity, in our solemnest thanksgivings. Only he that has no need of this visit, no need of Christ or his redemption, that cares not to be saved, needs keep no Christmas, may stand out, or sit, or do what he will, at his Benedictus.
>
> But, sure, when all things else thus come in throngs to bless him, and even ice and snow come hot and eager to this feast, and willingly melt themselves into his praises, we should not, methinks, come coldly on to bless him, but come and bring our families and children and neighbours with us, to make the choir as full as possibly we can. Tell one another what Christ did today, what he every day does for us; how he visited us today, how he still visits us every morning; how he redeemed us today, how he does day by day, from one ill or other; how he began today to raise up salvation for us, and will not leave raising it for us till we can rise no higher. Tell we our children next, how in this God had respect to David his anointed, and that they must learn to have so. How he had regard to David his servant; will have so to them if they be his servants: let them therefore be sure they be so; fit them thus to sing their parts betimes in hymns, and anthems, and praises to their God; that they that cannot speak, may yet lisp it out; and when they can speak out, sing it loud and shrill, that the hollow vaults and arches may echo and rebound his praises: not your children only, but stones also be thus raised up for children unto Abraham.[14]

In this way, in humankind, the praises of animate and inanimate nature are joined together. All things centre themselves on human beings, and work together for their good, when they are fulfilling their vocation of acting towards God on behalf of all things. Each human being is a little world, and there is that in each which answers to all the changes and variety in the world around him. The vision so wonderfully expressed in the poetry of George Herbert, above all in the poem called simply 'Man', here finds in prose a no less eloquent exposition. In a passage where he insists on the part played by the human body as well as by the soul, Frank describes this correspondence very fully.

And of the seasons there are some, you know, more acceptable than others; two very acceptable and pleasant in the year, the spring and the summer. There are the same in the souls of men; a spring, when our graces and virtues begin to sprout and blossom, bespread and clothe this earth we carry; when the Sun of Righteousness begins to smile and warm us; when the air grows temperate, our passions and affections moderate within us, and all our powers breathe nothing but violets and roses; this, as the prophet styles it, 'the very time of love'; a disposition and a time we cannot but be accepted in, wherein God begins to be in love with us. There is a summer too, when 'the hills' – the highest pitch and spirit of our souls – 'stand thick with corn', and 'the valleys' – our lowest powers, our inferior passions – 'laugh and sing'; when the bright rays of heaven shine hot upon us; when we are hung full with all heavenly fruits; when our hearts do even 'burn within us', and the whole desires even of our flesh, this dust that covers us, are on fire for heaven; when our hearts 'pant after the living brooks', and our 'souls are athirst for God', to come unto him, to 'appear before him'. This, indeed, is not only the time, but the fullness of it; when, coming so replenished with grace and righteousness, we shall be fully accepted, and be sure not to be sent empty away.[15]

It is indeed striking in this passage to see how the images of spring and summer are used to describe the development of human life, our joy in being, and knowing ourselves to be, children of God.

Not only our higher faculties are fulfilled, 'our lowest powers, our inferior passions' rejoice as well. Nothing is to be left out, all has a part to play in the harmony of the whole. All is created by God, all is redeemed in Christ. As we shall see, when we come to look at Mark Frank's sermons on our Lady, this thought plays an important part in his understanding of her blessedness.

We have seen enough of the preaching of Mark Frank to be able to perceive that he stands in the tradition of Hooker and Andrewes, and rejoices to affirm the faith of the wholeness of the Christian tradition. Preaching on Christmas Day on the text from Psalm 45, 'Thou art fairer than the children of men', and applying the words to Christ, he says,

> The Fathers have so expounded it before us; the Church has added the authority to it by the choice of the Psalm for a part of the Office of the Day; nay, St Paul has so applied it. So I am in no ways singular; indeed I love not to be in such points as these; I tread the ancient track; though I confess I think I can never take occasions enough – not I, nor any else – to speak of Christ, of his beauty and grace and blessedness, either today or any day, though every day whatsoever.[16]

And then at once, having evoked the authority of the Fathers, he brings forward one of the fundamental qualities of all their approach to the things of God, saying 'with St Hilary, *Filium mens mea veretur attingere, et trepidat omnis sermo se prodere,* I can neither think without a kind of fear, nor speak without a kind of trembling, of a person of that glory.'[17] This appeal to the authority of the Fathers is not a mere matter of external conformity. It implies thinking with them, feeling with them, sharing their own amazement before the mystery of the divine in the human, the human in the divine.

In an Easter sermon, when he is applying the verse of Psalm 118, 'This is the day which the Lord hath made . . .' to the matter of feasts, he cites Andrewes explicitly, 'And of this day of the resurrection, the Fathers, the Church, the Scriptures understand it. Not one of the Fathers, says that devout and learned Bishop Andrewes, that he had read, (and he had read many), but interpret it of Easter-day.' And Frank brings forward the evidence of the

liturgy to show how the mind of the Church has shaped itself. 'The
Church picks out this Psalm today, as a piece of service proper to it.
This very verse in particular, was anciently used every day in Easter
week; evidence enough how she understood it.'[18]

The affirmation which is implicit in such remarks of the value
of unity and tradition for understanding the Christian faith and
fully entering into the Christian life comes out very clearly in
the Third Sermon on Whitsunday. Frank asserts that it is the
Scripture which provides the primary way by which the Spirit
leads us into all truth. But, he says, not the Scripture alone for

> this may all men pretend to, and everyone turns it how he lists.
> We must add a second. And the second is the Church, for we
> must know this, says St Peter; know it first too – that no
> Scripture is of any private interpretation. . . When men unlearned
> or ungrounded, presume to be interpreters, or even learned men
> to prefer their private senses before the received ones of the
> Church, it is never like to produce better. The 'pillar' and
> 'ground' upon which truth stands and stays is the Church, if
> St Paul may be allowed to be the judge.[19]

And the Church to which Frank makes appeal is no invisible
or notional body. It is the Church of all the centuries.

> Indeed in itself it is most ridiculous to think the custom, and
> practice and order, and interpretation of all times and Churches
> should be false, and those of yesterday only true, unless we can
> think the Spirit of truth has been fifteen or sixteen hundred years
> asleep, and never waked till now of late; or can imagine that
> Christ should found a Church, and promise to be with it to the
> end of the world, and then leave it presently to Antichrist to be
> guided by him for above fifteen hundred years together.[20]

For Frank there can be no question but that we must constantly
appeal to 'the Scriptures interpreted by the perpetual practice of
God's Church', if we are to maintain the balance and proportion
of the faith. Like all the seventeenth-century Anglicans he recognized
a certain primacy in the witness of the Scriptures to the original apostolic tradition, which enabled the Church to perceive if, in the

course of centuries, faith or practice had gone radically out of true. In this sense, he is and remains, on the Reformation side of the sixteenth-century division. But as we have seen in the passages cited, he was aware that the appeal to Scripture alone, could leave the Christian people at the mercy of the whims and fancies of arbitrary interpretations, from whence have come so many Christian divisions. For him, therefore, the only sure way to approach the Scriptures is through the tradition, to read them in the light of the faith and worship of the Christian centuries, with the assistance of the reflection of the Fathers and Councils.[21] It is in this way that he approaches the question of the place of Mary in the scheme of redemption, and seeks to find a position of balance between the then violently opposed positions of Rome and Protestantism.

It is against this background of bitter controversy that we can best appreciate the achievement of Mark Frank's teaching on this topic. To speak of bitter controversy in this connection is no exaggeration. Passions were often violent, and feelings ran high particularly on anything to do with the veneration of Mary. One of the charges brought against Archbishop Laud at his trial was that he had caused a statue of our Lady to be put up over the porch of the university church of St Mary in Oxford. In such a context we can evaluate something of the boldness of Frank's treatment of this subject. It combines a powerful and daring eloquence with a careful and balanced judgement. While he does not hesitate to castigate the Puritan neglect of all mention of the Mother of the Lord, he also never forgets the proportion of faith, as he sees it set out in Scripture. In his sermon on the Feast of the Annunciation which contains his fullest treatment of the subject, he makes this point very clearly, and it is one which we should do well to note at the outset.

From Christ's being with her and with us, it is that we are blessed. From his incarnation begins the dawn of our happiness. If God be not with us, all the world cannot make us happy, much less blessed. From this grace of his incarnation first riseth all our glory; so that 'Not unto us, O Lord, not unto us, but unto thy name give the praise', must she sing as well as we; and they do her wrong as well as God, that give his glory unto her, who will not give his glory to another, though to his mother, because she is but his earthly mother – a thing infinitely distant from the heavenly Father. Nor would that humble handmaid, if she should understand the vain and fond and almost idolatrous styles and honours that are given her somewhere upon earth, be pleased with them; she is highly favoured enough that her Lord and Son is with her, and she with him; she would be no higher sharer.[22]

But if Mary is never to be confused with God, always to be seen as one who draws all her grace and glory from God, she is nevertheless one who is highly, uniquely favoured, one who is, in a certain sense, the place where God is to be found, one whose childbearing stands at the very centre of the Church's life. This point is brought out very vividly in a passage from one of the sermons for Epiphany, where Frank is commenting on the coming of the Magi, who enter the house and see the young child with Mary his mother and fall down and worship him.

I do not wonder interpreters make this house the church of God. It is the gate and court of heaven, now Christ is here; angels sing round about it; all holiness is in it, now Christ is in it; here all creatures, reasonable and unreasonable, come to pay their homage to their Creator; hither they come even from the ends of the earth, to their devotions; a 'house of prayer' it is 'for all people', Gentiles and all; hither they come to worship, hither they come to pay their offerings and their vows; here is the shrine and altar, the glorious Virgin's lap, where the Saviour of the world is laid to be adored and worshipped; here stands the star for tapers to give light; and here the wise men this day become the priests – worship and offer, present prayers and praises, for themselves, and the whole world besides, all people of the world, high and low, learned and ignorant, represented by them.[22]

It is a remarkable paragraph. In the first place it shows his strong sense of the significance of the liturgical year. In the worship of the Church the mystery commemorated becomes a present reality. God is with us, in our midst. The Church's liturgy involves much more than a simple remembering of the past. Then, further, we see that his presence and manifestation in the world acts as a power for reintegration, drawing together all people, all creation around this centre of light. But Mary's part is not less striking for she also is at its centre; not herself the object of worship and adoration, but the altar, the shrine, the holy place where God is to be found.

Of the six sermons preached on Christmas Day, there is only one which speaks directly and at length of the rôle of Mary in the mystery of the incarnation, and this in itself gives an indication of the kind of proportion which Mark Frank tried to preserve. But the second sermon in which these references occur is certainly among his finest utterances. The text is Luke 2:2. 'And she brought forth her first-born son, and wrapped him in swaddling clothes, and laid him in a manger; because there was no room for them in the inn.' The sermon opens abruptly with a shout of praise and thanksgiving.

> I shall not need to tell you who this 'she', or who this 'him'. The day rises with it in its wings. This day wrote it with the first ray of the morning sun upon the posts of the world. The angels sung it in their choir, the morning stars together in their courses. The Virgin Mother, the Eternal Son. The most blessed among women, the fairest of the sons of men. The woman clothed with the sun: the sun compassed with a woman. She the gate of heaven: he the King of Glory that came forth. She the mother of the everlasting God: he God without a mother; God blessed for evermore. Great persons as ever met upon a day.[24]

But as we saw in Jeremy Taylor, this greatness and glory is hidden and not apparent. This is the theme of the whole sermon. 'Yet as great as the persons, and as great as the day, the great lesson of them both is to be little, to think and make little of ourselves; seeing the infinite greatness in this day become so little. Eternity as a child, the rays of glory wrapped in rags, Heaven crowded into the corner of a stable, and He that is everywhere want room.' The sermon is one of paradox and fruitfulness, of mysteriousness and new life, as if to emphasize that it is when the opposites come together that something new can come to birth. And what is true primarily of Mary and her Son, is true also in a measure of each one of us, for we are to 'suffer him to be born in us, who was born for us'. 'It is a day of bringing forth; sure, then, there is no being barren.'[25]

In this mysterious act, Frank says, all the unfolding of the scheme of salvation is present in little in the very beginning: '. . . the cross made up or involved in his cratch, (for of the form of a cross the cratch, some say, was made), man's salvation in God's incarnation, the Church's growth in the Virgin's bringing forth, many brethren in the First-born among them.'[26] We could hardly have a more concise statement of the way in which the whole of the economy of the Church has its roots in the childbearing of Mary. We are reminded of Andrewes's remarks about the font as the womb of the Church. And all Frank seems to say is wrapped in paradox ... 'his Godhead in the manhood, the Word in flesh, eternity in days, righteousness in a body like to a body of sin, wisdom in the infancy of a child, abundance in poverty, glory in disrespect, the fountain of grace in a dry, barren, dusty land, eternal light in clouds, and the everlasting life in the very image of death.'[27] The Fathers themselves could not underline further the paradoxes of the incarnation and redemption.

And here all is of a piece, all follows in this sacramental way. The whole gospel, Frank maintains,

> was wrapped up in clothes that seeing we might see and not presently understand, a mystery kept secret since the world began; his doctrine wrapped in parables, his grace covered in the sacraments, the inward grace in the outward elements, his great apostolic functions in poor simple fishermen, his Universal Church in a few obscure disciples in Judaea, the height of his knowledge in the simplicity of faith, the excellency of his precepts in the plainness of his speech, and the glory of the end they drive to in the humility of the way they lead. Well may the prophet exclaim, *Vere tu es Deus absconditus!* 'Verily thou art a God that hidest thyself', O God of Israel, the Saviour![28]

As at the end of most of his festival sermons, so at the end of this one, Frank follows the example of his master, Andrewes, and applies the whole matter of his exhortation directly to the Eucharist, which is about to be celebrated, leading his hearers' attention on to the altar of the church, the place where Christ is soon to be found. Although Mary is nowhere named in this passage, we are already familiar enough with Frank's method to know that the thought of her is not far away. It is she whom we must imitate if we are to welcome Christ into the stable of our lives. This paragraph, with its evocation not only of Bethlehem but of the festivities of an

English seventeenth-century Christmas, is very characteristic of its author. He is far from wishing to dissociate the sacred from the secular. He is not afraid to let heavenly mysteries be rooted even in the popular traditions of Christmas feasting, as long as they will open themselves in amazement to the overwhelming and paradoxical gratuity of God's action.

> What though there be no room for him in the inn? I hope there is in our houses for him. It is Christmas time, and let us keep open house for him; let his rags be our Christmas raiment, his manger our Christmas cheer, his stable our Christmas great chamber, hall, dining room. We must clothe with him, and feed with him, and lodge with him at this feast. He is now ready by and by to give us himself to eat; you may see him wrapped ready in the swaddling clothes of his blessed sacrament; you may behold him laid upon the altar as in his manger. Do but make room for him and we will bring him forth, and you shall look upon him and handle him, and feed upon him; bring me only the rags of a rent and torn and broken and contrite heart, the white linen cloths of pure intentions and honest affections to swathe him in, wrap him up fast, and lay him close to our souls and bosoms. It is a day of mysteries: it is a mysterious business we are about; Christ wrapped up, Christ in the sacrament, Christ in a mystery; let us be content to let it go so, believe, admire and adore it.[29]

What is implicit in the sermons for Christmas and Epiphany becomes explicit in the single sermon for the Feast of the Annunciation which we must now consider. Frank takes for his text the angel's salutation, 'And the angel came in unto her and said, Hail, thou that art highly favoured, the Lord is with thee: blessed art thou among women.' In his characteristic style he begins abruptly. 'The day will tell you who this "blessed among women" is: we call it our Lady-day; and the text will tell you why she comes into the day, because the Angel came in to her. And the Angel will tell you why he today came in to her; she was "highly favoured" and "the Lord was with her", was to come himself this day in to her, to make her "the most blessed among women".'[38] As before, Frank chooses to make use of the popular name for the feast, Lady-day, in order to begin his exposition of its meaning; like Andrewes he enjoys teasing out the different meanings of simple phrases, drawing his doctrine from elementary forms of speech, preaching, we may suppose, to a congregation in which people of very different levels of education were gathered.

His whole exposition here is centred upon the words *Dominus tecum*, 'The Lord is with thee'. Everything either follows from it, or leads towards it. Even the apparently incidental fact that the feast falls in Lent, and that this might seem inappropriate, is seen in this context. With a sharp intuition into the value of fasting, he says, 'It is the very time for *gratia plena*, to be filled when we are empty; the only time for *Dominus tecum*, for our Lord's being with us, when we have most room to entertain him.'[31] It is when we know ourselves to be poor and empty that God can come. As he remarks later in the sermon, 'It was the humility of his handmaid that God, in this high favour of the Incarnation of his Son, respected in her. Humility the ground of all grace within us – all grace without us, – of God's grace to us, – of his grace in us – the very grace that graces them all.'[32] Mary's blessedness, her glory, lies above all things in her humility. She points us always to the one who comes to her, who comes in her. It is this which enables the preacher to maintain that balance or proportion of faith, which he so much admires and which he feels is threatened both by those who disparage or ignore her, and by those whose veneration for her runs to an exaggeration which defeats its own ends.

> Indeed *Dominus tecum* is the chief business; the Lord Christ's being with her, that which the Church especially commemorates in the day. Her being 'blessed' and all our being 'blessed', 'highly favoured', or favoured at all, either men or women being so, all our hail, all our health and peace and joy, all the angels' visits to us, or kind words, all our conferences with heaven, all our titles and honours in heaven and earth, that are worth naming, come only from it. For *Dominus tecum* cannot come without them; he cannot come to us but we must be so, must be highly favoured in it, and blessed by it. So the Incarnation of Christ, and the Annunciation of the Blessed Virgin – his being incarnate of her, and her blessedness by him, all our blessedness in him with her, make it as well our Lord's as our Lady's day. More his, because his being Lord made her a Lady, else a poor carpenter's wife,

God knows; all her worthiness and honour, as all ours, is from him; and we to take heed today, or any day, of parting them; or so remembering her as to forget him; or so blessing her as to take away any of our blessing him; and of his worship to give to her. Let her blessedness, the respect we give her, be *inter mulieres*, 'among women' still; such as is fit and proportionate to weak creatures, not due and proper only to the Creator, that *Dominus tecum*, Christ in her be the business: that we take pattern by the Angel, to give her no more than is due to her, yet to be sure to give her that though, and that particularly upon the day.[33]

Frank is well aware of the difficulties of this theme. In the context of his own time in which the subject had been one of such violent controversy, there was much to be said for leaving it in silence. Indeed he may also have felt a deeper reason for reticence before this mystery, a sense that here are subjects which are fit more for inner meditation than for public exposition. Yet it is the very needs of his time which force him to speak out. Where the faith is distorted or exaggerated, ignored or derided, it is necessary to try to restore the balance, and to find the true proportion. And this point about the Mother of the Lord which is apparently a secondary one, is in fact intimately related to the very heart of the Christian affirmation, that God and humankind are reconciled in Christ.

Nor should I scarce, I confess, have chosen such a theme today, though the Gospel reach it me, but that I see it is time to do it, when our Lord is wounded through our Lady's sides, both our Lord and the mother of our Lord, most vilely spoken of by a new generation of wicked men, who, because the Romanists make little less of her than a goddess, they make not so much of her as a good woman; because they bless her too much, these unbless her quite, at least will not suffer her to be blessed as she should.[34]

In dealing with this subject, Frank then closely follows the text of St Luke, basing all his exposition on that, but at the same time turning for guidance to the Fathers. In this case it is the more remarkable that he does so because he may himself have felt uneasy at some of the ways in which they develop the theme. As before, it is not only the early Fathers who are cited, but also

St Bernard (or at least sermons then attributed to him), St Peter Damian and Hugh of St Victor. In this he simply follows the practice of Lancelot Andrewes, who frequently cites St Bernard alongside the teachers of the fourth century. If Frank felt any reserves about some aspects of their Mariology, he says nothing of them in the course of the sermon, but quotes them as authorities together with St Jerome and St Ambrose.

We find recurring in the sermon many of the themes with which we are already familiar in Andrewes and Taylor. There is for instance the comparison of Mary with the angels. Having spoken of Gabriel, the angel of the annunciation, and given various patristic interpretations of the meaning of his name, Frank says, 'So we have done with him; come we now to her – a greater than he – if we may speak with Epiphanius and some others.'[35] Or again there is the thought of Mary as the type and model of the life of contemplation, 'If we look for angels' company and salutations, we must be much within. "A garden enclosed is my sister, my spouse; a spring shut up, a fountain sealed," says Christ. The spouse of Christ, the soul he loves and vouchsafes his company, much private, oft within – within and at her prayers and meditation too. So was the blessed Virgin (say the Fathers here), blessedly employed, watching at her devotions . . .'[36] In both cases, if we are to find the language more than picturesque and baffling we must reflect on all that the inner journey of humankind involves, the hazards and the achievements; and must consider that the central affirmation of the union of God with humanity in Christ implies that none of the forces of the inner or the outer world, however apparently powerful they may be, can separate us from the love of God in Christ. In the union of human with divine in Christ something of still greater significance has occurred. Only in the light of the redemptive incarnation can we begin to see the meaning of this tradition about the service of the angels.

So the preacher comes to the terms of the angelic salutation: Hail, Ave. 'It speaks joy and peace and health, and salvation, both to her, and to us by her . . .'[37] for we all are involved in this salutation. He examines in detail the meaning of Gabriel's form of address. He assures us that he will not give Mary styles and titles other than those contained in Scripture; there is to be no equalling her with God. But at the same time, we are not to think simply to equal her with ourselves, however much we may remember her sharing our creatureliness.

> We are not to salute great persons by their names, but by their titles; and the Mother of God is above the greatest we meet with upon earth. We must not be too familiar with those whom God so highly favours; that is our lesson hence. We are not to speak of the Blessed Virgin, the Apostles and Saints, as if we were speaking to our servants, Paul, Peter, Mary or the like. It is a new fashion of religion, neither taken from saints, nor angels, nor any of heaven or heavenly spirits, to unsaint the saints, to deny them their proper titles, to level them with the meanest of our servants.[38]

Again he turns to the Fathers, to fill out his interpretation. The name Mary is 'high and illustrious' he tells us.

> Maria is *maris stella*, says St Bede: 'the star of the sea'; a fit name for the mother of the bright Morning Star that rises out of the vast sea of God's infinite and endless love. Maria, the Syriac interprets *domina*, 'a lady', a name yet retained and given to her by all Christians; our Lady, or the Lady Mother of our Lord. Maria, rendered by Petrus Damiani, *de monte et altitudine Dei*, highly exalted as you would say, like the mountain of God, in which he would vouchsafe to dwell, after a more miraculous manner than in very Sion, his 'own holy mount'. St Ambrose interprets it, *Deus ex genere meo*, 'God of my kin'; as if by her very name she was designed to have God born of her, to be *deipara*, as the Church, against all heretics, has ever styled her the Mother of God.[39]

It is in this context that, having earlier affirmed the solidarity between Mary and all believers, he can also confidently assert the uniqueness of her calling, a uniqueness which yet includes us all within itself.

> He is not with her, as he is with any else. *Tecum in mente, tecum in ventre*, as the Fathers gloss it; *Tecum in spiritu, tecum in carne*, with her he was, or would be presently, as well in

her body as in her soul, personally, essentially, nay bodily with her, and take a body from her – a way of being with any never heard before or since, – a being with her beyond any expression or conception whatsoever. And the Lord thus being with her, all good must needs be with her: all gracious ways of his being with us are comprehended in it; so the salutation no way exceeded. And well may he choose to be with her – even make haste and prevent the Angel, as St Bernard speaks, to be with her. He is with 'the pure in heart', with the humble spirit and piously retired soul, and she is all.[40]

From the theological point of view, one of the most interesting passages in the sermon is that where he discusses the meaning of the words *gratia plena*: 'highly favoured', 'full of grace'. The two translations sum up in themselves one of the crucial controversies of the sixteenth and seventeenth centuries. Is God's grace his unmerited favour towards us, *favor Dei*, or is it a supernatural gift which he implants in us, *gratia infusa*? As we have seen, it is fundamental to Frank's position that all the blessedness of Mary is of God's pure gift. It is noteworthy that he nowhere in this sermon uses the language of 'merit'. In this sense he belongs to the Reformation side of the controversy. Grace is not primarily a quality which we possess. It is the name for a relationship initiated by God. But to say this is not necessarily to deny the other interpretation, for this relationship with God is a transforming relationship, which creates anew the one who is drawn into it. So we find that Frank refuses to recognize a necessary opposition between the two approaches. Having assured the primacy of God's action, he happily equates the two. ' "Thou that art highly favoured", so our translation renders it: "full of grace"; so our old hath it, from the Latin, *gratia plena*; and both right; for it will carry both. Grace is favour; God's grace is divine favour; high in grace, high in his favour; full of his grace, full of his favour – all comes to one.'[41] It is a remarkable affirmation in face of the bitter controversies of the time.

Where he is concerned to make the distinctions is between 'sanctifying and edifying' grace, 'the gifts of the Holy Spirit that sanctify and make us holy; or the gifts that make us serviceable to make others so.' Here he is anxious to reject a view which will give Mary so much as to take her totally out of the human context, which will make it impossible to compare her with other saints. Like Taylor he insists that she has her own proper excellence, but not the excellence of others.

> Of each kind she had her fullness according to her measure, and the designation that God appointed her. For sanctifying graces, none fuller, *solo Deo excepto*, 'God only excepted', saith Epiphanius. And it is fit enough to believe that she who was so highly honoured to have her womb filled with the body of the Lord, had her soul as fully filled by the Holy Ghost.
> For edifying graces, as they came not all into her measure, she was not to preach, to administer, to govern, to play the apostle, and therefore no necessity she should be full of all those gifts, being those are not distributed all to any, but ... to everyone according to his measure and employment. . . Where any edifying grace was necessary for her, she had it as well as others; more perhaps than others. When it was not necessary, it was no way to the impairing of her fullness, though she had it not.[42]

As we might expect from Frank's treatment of the idea of blessing which we have already seen, it is when he comes to speak of Mary as blessed that his eloquence reaches its fullest pitch. It is a passage which is interesting in many ways. Considered biblically, it combines Old and New Testament allusions, the blessings promised to faithful Israel in Deuteronomy 28, together with a reference to the crucial verses, Luke 11:27-28, where in reply to the woman who cries out 'Blessed is the womb that bore thee', Jesus declares, 'Yea, rather blessed are they who hear the word of God and keep it.' They are interpreted here as the Evangelist surely meant them to be, as not pointing away from Mary, but to the true nature of her blessedness who 'kept all these things and pondered them in her heart'. At the same time, and by way of the Old Testament, the passage takes up the idea of the fruitfulness of creation, the good earth open to God's grace and mercy which shower down from heaven upon it. The notion of the human being as a microcosm has a very special relevance here, for Mary may be seen as herself the land of promise, at the heart and centre of the creation, as it turns itself towards God. The circling of the seasons as well as the history of God's choice of a particular people find their fulfilment in her bringing forth. "All creation rejoices in thee', the Eastern Church sings to the Mother of God. Mark Frank in his preaching makes the affirmation no less clearly.

> From this follows the second title, 'blessed', blessed of God, blessed of man; blessed in the city, and blessed in the field. Cities and countries call her blessed; blessed in the fruit of her body, and her blessed child Jesus. Blessed in the fruit of her ground, her cattle, her kine, and her sheep, in the inferior faculties of her soul and body; all fructify to Christ. Blessed her basket and her store, her womb and her breasts; the womb that bare him, and the paps that gave him suck. Blessed in her going out and her coming in, the Lord still being with her; the good treasure of heaven still open to her, showering down upon her, and the earth filled with the blessings which she brought forth into the world, when she brought forth the Son of God. Blessed she indeed that was the conduit of so great blessings, though blessed most in the bearing him in her soul, much more than bearing him in her body. So Christ intimates to the woman that began to 'bless the womb', that is, the mother 'that bare him'; 'Yea rather,' says he, 'blessed they that hear the word of God and keep it'; as if he had said, She is more blessed in bearing the word in her soul than in her body.[43]

We feel, in such a passage, how much our Christianity has lost by not being truly rooted in the material order, by not allowing the receptive side of our humanity, which is often thought to be particularly feminine, to enter fully into our mode of experience and our manner of thought. Frank opens to us the possibility of reappropriating part of the tradition, and, what is more, part of ourselves. The whole creation of which we are part can become for us the burning bush, on fire with the glory of the divinity yet not consumed, as we learn to receive it wholly as the gift of God. It is precisely because he sees Mary at the centre of this creation that Frank puts an absolute negative against any temptation to translate her to the side of the Creator. Her blessedness is full, but it is always 'a blessedness compatible to the creature'.

So once again he cautions against a distorted attitude towards her, seeking to find the true proportion of faith.

Give we her in God's name the honour due to her. God hath styled her 'blessed' by the angel, by Elizabeth; commanded all generations to call her so, and they hitherto have done it, and let us do it too. Indeed some of late have overdone it; yet let us not therefore underdo it, but do it as we hear the angel and the first Christians did it; account of her and speak of her as the most blessed among women, one 'highly favoured', most 'highly' too. But all the while give *Dominus tecum*, all the glory, the whole glory of all to him; give her the honour and blessedness of the chief of saints, – him only the glory that she is so, and that by her conceiving and bringing our Saviour into the world we are made heirs, and shall one day be partakers of the blessedness she enjoys, when the Lord shall be with us too, and we need no angel to tell us so.[44]

It is in relation to the coming of Christ that Mary's glory is truly to be seen. And she who stands at the centre of creation stands also at the centre of the company of those who believe, as in the Eastern icons of the Ascension and Pentecost she is seen standing in the midst of the apostolic band. She is the type of every Christian in whom the Lord is to be born,

especially if we now here dispose ourselves by chastity, humility, and devotion, as she did, to receive him, and let him be new born in us. The pure and virgin soul, the humble spirit, the devout affection will be also highly favoured; the Lord be with them and bless them above others. Blessed is the virgin soul, more blessed than others in St Paul's opinion; blessed the humble spirit above all. For God hath exalted the humble and meek, the humble handmaid better than the proudest lady. Blessed the devout affection that is always watching for her Lord in prayer and meditations; none so happy, so blessed as she; the Lord comes to none so soon as such.

It is some measure of the imbalance of male and female elements within us, and in our society, that we may feel a certain unease to find that for Frank these virtues of the woman should have necessarily to characterize *all* who believe in God. The vision of Christ as our mother, which occurs so naturally in Julian of

Norwich, the expectation that men should feel a motherly tenderness towards one another, which we find in St Francis, or the early Cistercian writers, such things demand a situation in which it is accepted that everyone carries the male and the female, *animus* and *amina*, within himself or herself and that any fullness of life demands their reconciliation. It is a vision which we greatly need to rediscover, and which much now urges us to find again for our health and the health of our whole society. Frank at least is quite clear on this point in his final affirmation.

In the concluding paragraphs of his sermon where he turns directly to the eucharist, he prays that 'we also may become Marys, and the mothers of our Lord'. In this final section we can see something of a coming together of all the themes we have been studying: Christ's presence in the flesh through the childbearing of blessed Mary, as the foundation of his presence in the Church, in each Christian, and in the Holy Communion, which thus becomes the focal point of the mystery of God's presence among his people, the centre of celebration for humankind and for all things.

The Lord comes, he declares, to none

> more fully than in the blessed Sacrament to which we are now agoing. There he is strangely with us, highly favours us, exceeding blesses us; there we are all made blessed Marys, and become mothers, sisters, and brothers of our Lord, while we hear his word, and conceive it in us; while we believe him who is the Word, and receive him too into us. There angels come to us on heavenly errands, and there our Lord indeed is with us, and we are blessed, and the angels hovering all about us to peep into those holy mysteries, think us so, call us so. There graces pour down in abundance on us – there grace is in its fullest plenty – there his highest favours are bestowed upon us – there we are filled with grace unless we hinder it, and shall hereafter in the strength of it be exalted into glory – there to sit down with this blessed Virgin and all the saints and angels, and sing praise, and honour, and glory, to him, Father, Son and Holy Ghost, for ever and ever.[45]

Taylor in his meditations and Frank in his sermons write about Mary in a rich and elaborate style notable for its abundant use of imagery. Very different is the approach of their contemporary, Herbert Thorndike (1598-1672). Thorndike is perhaps the most rigorous and systematic of seventeenth-century Anglican theologians. Not that the system always appears on the surface of his writings, for they abound in digressions and asides and in general lack the literary quality which makes reading the seventeenth-century writers such a pleasure. At times Thorndike can be obscure, at times full of insight, but a careful reading of his work reveals a theological vision of remarkable unity and consistency.

> ... His mature writings, products of enforced leisure during the 1650s, very consciously proceed from theological first principles (questions of method and interpretation, for instance), on to an explication of the economy of salvation (chiefly the doctrine of the incarnation, but integral to it, Trinitarian theology and pneumatology) and conclude in its outworking in the life of the people of God individually and corporately (the sacraments, polity, church order, etc.).[46]

His view of the economy of salvation is trinitarian through and through. It makes much of the complementarity and reciprocity of the action of the Word and the Spirit. It sees the climax of the drama of salvation in Christ's life-giving victory over death, a climax which leads directly to the Ascension and the gift of the Spirit at Pentecost. The life of the Church, and of each member of it, flows out from these mysteries through the sacraments of baptism and eucharist in which both Easter and Pentecost are made present and renewed.

Here is a pattern of doctrine which follows on and systematizes lines opened up by Lancelot Andrewes. It clearly owes much to Thorndike's massive knowledge of the fathers, and it has interesting parallels with twentieth-century Orthodox theologians such as Vladimir Lossky. Its overall pattern is strikingly different from the typical christocentric model of theology focused on a forensic doctrine of the atonement which for centuries came to be characteristic of the West, both Catholic and Protestant. It is strongly resistant to that kind of theism which tends to reify God 'reducing infinite mystery to an independent existing Supreme Being alongside other beings, a solitary transcendent power who together with the world can be thought to form a larger whole'.[47] One of the most impressive and interesting features of Thorndike's system is the emphasis it gives to catholic consent, the agreement of East and West, of Rome and the Reformation, in the central affirmations of Christian faith. For him everything centres on the witness of the Scriptures as interpreted by the perpetual practice of Christ's Church. In this scheme of things Mary has a quantitively small but nevertheless vital place. Characteristically for the Anglicans of his time, his thought about her centres on the moment of the Annunciation.

Thorndike's major work was published at the end of the Commonwealth period of 1659. Its title at once makes its ecumenical intention evident: *The Epilogue to the Tragedy of the Church of England, being a necessary Consideration and brief Resolution of the chief Controversies in Religion that divide the western Church. . .*[48] It is divided into three treatises: I) *The Principles of Christian Truth*; II) *The Covenant of Grace*; III) *The Laws of the Church*. Thorndike's consideration of the Annunciation comes into the second treatise and forms part of his defence of the classical doctrine of the incarnation against the attacks of the Socinians. In this context, Thorndike is particularly concerned to reaffirm the patristic understanding of the theophanies of the Old Testament as already implicitly trinitarian. Angelic messengers as ambassadors of God are sent to God's people bearing God's word.

> For, as I said afore, that when it is said in the Old Testament that 'the Word of God came' to this or that prophet, an angel appeared unto him, speaking in the person of God, who was therefore worshipped as God, because the Word of God . . . was in that angel at the present for that service; so I must further note here that on such Word of God coming to a prophet he became inspired, that is possessed and acted, by the spirit of God, for the time of that service which God by such a message employed him about.[49]

The Annunciation is seen as at once the climax of the history of God's dealings with his people and as the transition to something altogether new. Here there is not a transitory possession of the human by the divine, but a permanent and transforming indwelling. Here the action of the Word and the Spirit become explicit. Thorndike insists that in the Word the Spirit is present. His christology is powerfully trinitarian.

> When therefore the angel Gabriel appeared to the blessed virgin saying, 'The Holy Ghost shall come upon thee and the Most High shall overshadow thee, and therefore the Holy Thing that is born . . . shall be called the Son of God', we are to understand, that the Holy Ghost . . . upon this message possessing the flesh of the blessed virgin made it a tabernacle for the Word of God always to dwell in; in which Word the Spirit of God always dwelt. For so the difference holds between our Lord Christ in whom dwells the fullness of the Spirit and his servants which have each of them his measure of it; if we understand the Word incarnate to have in it resident the presence of God's spirit, by which our Lord Christ proved himself the Son of God . . .[50]

A little further on, Thorndike insists again on the permanence of the divine indwelling of the Spirit and the humanity of the incarnate Word. In Christ all the fullness of the Godhead dwells bodily (Col.2: 9-10). This is nothing less than the indwelling of the Holy Trinity.

> The Holy Ghost overshadowing the blessed virgin, not only works the conception of a son, but dwells forever according to the fullness of the godhead in the manhood so conceived; as by the action of the godhead, planted in the Word which there came to dwell in the manhood so conceived. Therefore that holy thing which is born of the virgin being 'called the Son of God' is made so much above the angels as the esteem which his name imparts is above anything that is attributed to them in the scriptures.[51]
>
> For here it is much to be observed, that as St Paul affirmeth the fullness of the godhead to dwell bodily in Christ, because the Holy Ghost is understood always to be resident in the Word incarnate; so by the same reason the Father also is contained in the Son as the Son in the Father likewise.[52]

This pattern of trinitarian presence and activity characterizes the church at every level. Thorndike makes interesting use of the model of the Annunciation in relation to the consecration of the eucharist. For him it is the Holy Spirit who is active in the consecration.

> Now it is executed, and hath always been executed by the action of the church upon God's word of institution, praying that the Holy Ghost coming down upon the present elements 'may make them the body and blood of Christ', not by changing them into the nature of flesh and blood, as the bread and wine that nourished our Lord Christ upon earth became the flesh and blood of the Son of God, by becoming the flesh and blood of his manhood, hypostatically united to his godhead; saith St Gregory Nyssen; but immediately and *ipso facto* by being united to the spirit of Christ, that is his godhead.[53]

The Spirit which overshadows Mary at Nazareth overshadows the gathering of the church and overshadows the offerings which are placed on the altar. Like Lancelot Andrewes before him, Thorndike uses this analogy to argue against the doctrine of transubstantiation, by which the substance of the bread and wine was said to be abolished to make place for the substance of the body and blood. So in another place he can ask polemically, 'Was the flesh and blood of the blessed virgin abolished, that it might become the flesh and blood of our Lord?'[54]

If Thorndike can use the example of Mary in his argument against Rome so, of course, he can also use it in his argument against the Reformation. He does this when he defends the possibility that Christians may receive a calling to withdraw from this world and follow Christ in singleness and simplicity of life. If such a life is not possible,

> Then would not our Lord have encouraged it, then would not St Paul have advised virgins to it, then would not the church from the beginning have used and frequented it. The virginity of our Lord's mother as it is a warrant that the curse of barrenness by the law is turned into a blessing by the gospel, so has it an example for the church to follow. And this example, having been followed by all ages of the church, showed the effects of the promise.[55]

The very quietness of the last affirmation has something about it which demands our attention.

As we have seen the second major part of Thorndike's work is called *The Covenant of Grace*. The concept of covenant is fundamental in his theology as it was in that of his Puritan contemporaries but his understanding of the concept is very different from theirs. For although in Thorndike as in his Calvinist adversaries, everything comes from God and is the work of God's grace, Thorndike's understanding of this in no way excludes the free response of humankind. His is a theology of synergy, the co-operation of human and divine, in which human freedom is at every point supported and sustained by divine grace; so we are not surprised that he can make use of the early Christian contrast between the obedience of Mary and the disobedience of Eve, for Mary's free assent is essential to the incarnation.

> And so when Irenaeus calls the Virgin Mary the 'advocate of Eve', he that considers his words . . . shall find that he saith it not because she prayed for her but because she believed the angel's message and submitted to God's will and so became the means for saving all; though by our Lord Christ, who pleadeth even for her as well as for Eve.[56]

Here we have a very interesting example of Thorndike fighting on two fronts. For if on the one side he uses the example of Eve to show 'an example of that engraced and free obedience which through Christ and his Spirit humanity is once more able to bring to the divine-human relationship,'[57] on the other he is careful to maintain that it is not any independent prayer of Mary that makes her the advocate of Eve; all is through our Lord Christ 'who pleadeth even for her as well as for Eve'.

This passage is in fact part of a long and interesting discussion of the ways in which Christians should express their faith in the communion of saints in prayer and worship. Thorndike distinguishes three forms of prayer as used in the Roman Catholic Church of his time. The first consists of prayers addressed to God to hear us at or through the prayers of the saints (as in the canon of the Latin mass). These Thorndike considers to be wholly agreeable to our common Christianity and he is prepared to argue strongly for their restoration to the Book of Common Prayer. The third type consists of long prayers addressed directly to Our Lady and the saints asking them for earthly and heavenly blessings of all kinds. These, he says, if they are taken literally, are evidently idolatry. The fact that we recognize the church of Rome to be a true church, in his eyes tells us that we need not take them literally in this way. They must have other meanings than appear on the surface but this does not mean that they can be excused, let alone commended. In between these two forms are simple requests to the saints to pray for us. These are not in themselves objectionable, for to ask the saints to pray for us to God is evidently something different from praying to God himself. But despite their impressive patristic testimonies, Thorndike does not feel that they can be commended. He feels strongly that they can only too easily lead ordinary Christian people to give to creatures honours due to God alone; this is something which at all costs is to be avoided.[58]

A late twentieth-century Anglican, while profiting from the clarity of Thorndike's analysis, may well feel less anxious about prayers of the second and third type as long as their secondary rôle within the whole pattern of Christian prayer remains clearly established; as long, that is, as they do not enter into the heart of the eucharist or the sacramental rites of the church. The prayer of the Church is always and essentially trinitarian, made in the power of the Spirit through Jesus Christ to God the Father and Creator of all. But then in the twentieth century Anglicans are likely to have had practical experience of the Roman Catholic Church of kinds which were scarcely possible for their seventeenth-century predecessors. Thorndike only visited the continent once; a visit to Holland in search of a manuscript of Origen. He has all the northern European disgust for the fervent tactile emotional piety of the south, something partly religious, partly cultural. He cannot approve of prayers to the saints, he cannot approve of devotions to images. He is particularly shocked at the latter then they are supported by the clergy.

> What the effect of these excessive positions hath been is easy to see. They clothe their images, they paint them, they gild them the finest they may. They think themselves holy for touching, kissing,

and caressing them, as children do their babies [i.e. dolls]. They touch their bodies with them and think themselves hallowed by their means, they put a cotton on the end of a stick and touch first the images, then the eyes, the lips, the noses of those that come; *and that in their surplices*. [My italics]⁵⁹

It is ironical that this instinctive revulsion which lasted for four hundred years has begun to break up in the whole Reformation world in the last generation under the pressures of a new sense of the value of tactile, non-verbal means of communication and a new appreciation of the importance of gesture, movement, dance in the worship of God as well as in human relations. Whether or not these widespread tendencies can become a serious element in the movement for Christian unity is a matter for discussion. At least they remove some classical obstacles.

But if in some ways Thorndike is a typical Englishman of his century, an intellectual from the world of the Renaissance and Reformation, equipped with the latest scholarly resources of his time, there can be no doubt that as a theologian he is resolutely self-critical. He is willing to question the assumptions of the Protestant world and always ready to give full weight to the arguments on the other side. For instance, no other Anglican writer of his time makes so strong and convincing a case for the primacy of Rome, a primacy not absolute but nonetheless true, something which he sees as always to be used in the service of the catholic unity of all Christ's people. Similarly, though the space which he gives to Mary is not large, the place which she holds in his total understanding of theology cannot be ignored. It makes explicit what is often implicit in the preaching and meditations of many of his contemporaries. As Charles Miller concludes,

We can see now the place that Mary occupies within this theological vision. Her place is integral, unique, and paradigmatic at the same time. It is integral because it is developed within the framework of the doctrine of incarnation. It is unique because the Annunciation event was the occasion of a wholly particular, new relationship between human nature and the Spirit and the incarnate Word of God; it is paradigmatic because insofar as she received the Holy Spirit she then received the Word of God in her life. That experience then becomes paradigmatic for the church within the plan of salvation; through the perennial coming down of the Spirit at Pentecost, and forever after, believers are enabled to receive the Holy Spirit and thus give birth to the Word in their lives by faith.[60]

NOTES

1 Mark Frank, *Sermons*, Library of Anglo-Catholic Theology, vol. ii, p. 123
2 Ibid., i, p. 300
3 Ibid., ii, pp. 123-4
4 Aelred Squire, *Asking the Fathers* (1973), p. 56
5 A.L. Maycock, *Chronicles of Little Gidding* (London 1954), p.3
6 Ibid., i, pp. 340-1
7 Ibid., i, p. 5
8 Ibid., i, p. 191
9 Ibid., i, p. 192
10 Ibid., i, p. 55
11 Ibid., i, p. 223
12 Ibid., ii, p. 301
13 Ibid., i, p. 139
14 Ibid., i, p. 158-9
15 Ibid., i, pp. 381-2
16 Ibid., i, p. 126
17 Ibid., i, p. 126
18 Ibid., ii, p. 115
19 Ibid., ii, p. 234
20 Ibid., ii, p. 235
21 For an interesting study of the way in which Lancelot Andrewes handles this theme in his preaching, see the article by Nicholas Lossky, 'La patristique dans la prédication anglaise au début du xviie siècle; un exemple, Lancelot Andrewes' in *Messager de l'exarchat du patriarche russe en Europe occidentale*, nos. 105-8 (1980-1), pp. 113-21
22 Op. cit., ii, pp. 48-9
23 Ibid., i, p. 280

24 Ibid., i, p. 77
25 Ibid., i, pp. 89-91
26 Ibid., i, p. 86
27 Ibid., i, p. 86
28 Ibid., i, p. 87
29 Ibid., i, p. 90
30 Ibid., ii, p. 33
31 Ibid., ii, p. 34
32 Ibid., ii, p. 48
33 Ibid., ii, p. 34
34 Ibid., ii, pp. 35-6
35 Ibid., ii, p. 39
36 Ibid., ii, p. 41
37 Ibid., ii, p. 42
38 Ibid., ii, p. 45
39 Ibid., ii, pp. 32-40
40 Ibid., ii, pp. 43-4
41 Ibid., ii, pp. 45-6
42 Ibid., ii, p. 46
43 Ibid., ii, pp. 47-8
44 Ibid., ii, p. 50
45 Ibid., ii, pp. 50-1
46 Charles Miller, *Mary and the Eucharist: A Seventeenth-Century Anglican View* (Ecumenical Society of the BVM, 1992), p. 4. I am deeply grateful to my friend Father Charles Miller whose pamphlet alerted me to the importance of Thorndike's thought in this area. I am still more indebted to his doctoral thesis, E.C. Miller, *The Doctrine of the Church in the Thought of Herbert Thorndike*, presented in Oxford in 1990. This work, which unfortunately is not yet published, gives a masterly view of the inner coherence of Thorndike's theological system.
47 Elizabeth A. Johnson, *She Who Is: The Mystery of God in Feminist Theological Discourse*, (New York 1992), p. 20; cf. also p. 192
48 Published in the Library of Anglo-Catholic Theology, *The Theological Works of Herbert Thorndike*, vols. 3 and 4 (1849 and 1853)
49 Vol. 3, pp. 246-7

50 Ibid., p. 248
51 Ibid., pp. 253-4
52 Ibid., p. 257
53 Vol. 5, p. 173
54 Ibid., p. 545
55 Ibid., p. 539
56 Vol. 4, part 2, p. 771
57 Charles Miller, op. cit., p. 9
58 Vol. 4, part 2, pp. 761-84
59 Ibid., p. 795
60 Op. cit., p. 6

5

'The Whole Assembly Sings':
Thomas Traherne

We have examined so far the work of four seventeenth-century theologians, and sought to trace in them a number of closely related themes; the union of divine and human in Christ, the celebration of this mystery in the Church's liturgy, the redemption of the whole of human nature, and what this means in particular for the redemption of the body, and the place of Mary in this whole complex mystery. We must now look to another writer from a little later in the same century, in whom these different but related themes find a final and startling treatment. Final, because already in the years after the restoration of the monarchy the philosophical and scientific presuppositions which have made it possible to regard the human being as a microcosm were rapidly collapsing; startling, because here we are dealing with a writer with a peculiarly personal vision, and an ecstatic and incomparable style in which to convey it.

Thomas Traherne was not a professional theologian and teacher in the same way that Andrewes, Taylor, and Frank were. To outward appearances he was an undistinguished clergyman, first incumbent of Credenhill, a small parish near Hereford, then private chaplain to an influential courtier. Inwardly he was a man of penetrating vision, a poet alike in his prose and his verse. But it would be a mistake to think of him only as a poet and a man of imaginative vision. He was also a theologian concerned to show the coherence of his own particular insights with the pattern of the Christian faith taken as a whole. Certainly he had an astonishing recollection of the childhood experience of eternity and a powerful sense of the felicity of this world when the world is perceived as God's creation, filled with the energies of God's wisdom and God's love. This vision of the active presence of the divine Sophia-Wisdom, which is both aesthetic and theological, is particularly strong in the tradition of the Christian East. Here it receives an authentic and unself-conscious expression in the Christian West. It gives a peculiarly Sophianic radiant quality to Traherne's writing, a sense of the sacredness of the earth and all creation. He has a powerful perception of the way in which everything in creation, every atom of space and time can be open to the divine indwelling.

Because Traherne first came before the public at the beginning of this century as a writer of poetry and of richly imaginative prose, and since little enough was known of the external facts of his life, there has been a tendency to overlook the seriousness of his commitment to his work as a priest and a pastor at Credenhill. But among the writings still unpublished the *Select Meditations* in particular show him as a conscientious, almost over-anxious, parish priest. It is evident that some of these meditations date from the period immediately after the restoration of the monarchy, the time of Traherne's own episcopal ordination in 1660. Certificates of the church wardens at Credenhill, from the 1660s, recently discovered in the diocesan archives, reinforce this impression. A wider knowledge of his writing shows him to have been a man deeply attached to the liturgical tradition of the Church. The *Church's Yearbook*, another unpublished work, from which we shall quote extensively, is eloquent in this regard.[1] Certainly Traherne had his own unique point of vision. He develops the themes with which we are concerned in this book in his own specific way. But it is striking that they are interconnected in him exactly as they are in Andrewes, Taylor and Frank. As Deneef suggests in his remarkable study, there is an inner consistency and seriousness in Traherne's patterns of thought which has not always been recognized by those who comment on him.[2]

Whereas the writings which we have been dealing with in previous chapters have been little known and relatively inaccessible, some of the great passages in Traherne's *Centuries of Meditations* have become rightly famous and have passed into innumerable anthologies. Traherne's vision is his own, but his idea of humankind as created in God's image, rejoicing in all that God has made, is not in its substance very different from that which we find in Mark Frank. Inward and outward unite in the praise of God:

> You never enjoy the world aright, till the sea itself floweth in your veins, till you are clothed with the heavens, and crowned with the stars; and perceive yourself to be the sole heir of the whole world; and more than so, because men are in it who are every one sole heirs as well as you. Till you can sing and rejoice and delight in God, as misers do in gold, and kings in sceptres, you never enjoy the world.[3]

But what is often not recognized is that this sense of coinherence with the world has as its presupposition the faith that humankind is created in God's image, and that this image is restored and re-established in Christ. Contrary to the impression which many people have, Traherne's religion is not simply one of joy in creation. The theme of redemption appears powerfully in it, as a reading of the central chapters of the first *Century* shows.

> Would men consider what God hath done, they would be ravished in Spirit with the glory of his doings. For heaven and earth are full of the majesty of his glory. And how happy would men be could they see and enjoy it. But above all these our Saviour's cross is the throne of delights. That centre of eternity, that tree of life in the midst of the paradise of God... The cross of Christ is the Jacob's ladder by which we ascend into the highest heavens. There we see joyful patriarchs, expectant saints and prophets ministering, apostles publishing and doctors teaching. All nations concentring and angels praising. That cross is a tree set on fire with the invisible flame that illuminateth all the world. The flame is Love. The love in his bosom who died on it. In the light of which we see how to possess all the things in heaven and earth after his similitude.[4]

We should therefore greatly misunderstand Traherne if we thought of him simply as a solitary visionary. While he celebrates the inner riches of human life restored in God, in harmony with all created things, he is not unaware that this life has its outward social aspect, that things inward and outward are to rejoice together. So we can find in him, no less than in Andrewes and Frank, a celebration of the feast of Christ's nativity in which personal and social are joined together into one. In fact, in his poem 'Christmas-Day' we might say that something of the old undivided unity of Christendom, inward and outward, rich and poor, the world of nature and the world of humankind, Church and state together, finds expression, and Hereford becomes for an instant the image of the city, as the bells of the parish churches ring through the December air, and the mayor proceeds in state into the cathedral.

> See how, their bodies clad with finer clothes,
>   They now begin
>   His praise to sing
>   Who purchas'd their repose:
> Whereby their inward joy they do disclose:
> Their dress alludes to better works than those;
>   His gayer weeds and finer band,
>   New suit and hat, into his hand
>   The Plow-man takes, his neatest shoes,
>   And warmer gloves, he means to use:
>   And shall not I, my king
>   Thy praises sing.
>
> See how their breath doth smoke, and how they haste
>   His praise to sing
>   With cherubim;
>   They scarce a breakfast taste;
> But through the streets, lest precious time should waste,
> When service doth begin, to church they haste
>   And shall not I, Lord, come to thee,
>   The beauty of thy temple see?
>   Thy name with joy I will confess,
>   Clad in my Saviour's righteousness
>   'Mong all thy servants sing
>   To thee my king.
>
> 'Twas thou that gav'st us cause for fine attires;
>   Ev'n thou, O King,
>   As in the spring,

Dost warm us with thy fires
Of love; thy blood hath bought us new desires
Thy righteousness doth clothe with new attires.
   Made fresh and fine let me appear
   This day divine, to close the year;
   Among the rest let me be seen
   A living branch and always green,
      Think it a pleasant thing
         Thy praise to sing.

At break of day, O how the bells did ring!
      To thee, my King
      The bells did ring;
   To thee the angels sing;
Thy goodness did produce this other spring,
For this it is they make the bells to ring:
   The sounding bells do through the air
   Proclaim thy welcome far and near;
   While I alone with thee inherit
   All these joys, beyond my merit.
      Who would not always sing
         To such a King?

I, all these joys, above my merit, see
      By thee, my King,
      To whom I sing
   Entire, convey'd to me.
My treasure, Lord, thou mak'st the people be
That I with pleasure might thy servants see.
   Ev'n in their rude external ways
   They do set forth my Saviour's praise,
   And minister a light to me;
   While I by them do hear to thee
      Praises, my Lord and King,
         Whole churches sing.

Hark how remoter parishes do sound!
      Far off they ring
      For thee, my King,
      Ev'n round about the town;
The churches scattered over all the ground

Serve for thy praise, who art with glory crown'd.
  This city is an engine great
  That makes my pleasure more complete
  Thy sword, the mace, the magistrate
  To honour thee, attend in state
    The whole assembly sings;
      The Minster rings.[5]

    The poem is, as we say, an almost physical embodiment of what it is seeking to describe; the celebration of Christ's coming on the part of a whole Christian people. All the objects named in it play their part in the unity of the whole. But however fine the poetic achievement, we cannot overlook the deeply felt and understood theology which underlies it. Christmas is the celebration of Christ's nativity, therefore of the unity of humanity with God in him. In the darkness and cold of our human alienation from God and from our neighbour, a new and 'mid-winter' spring appears. The coldness of our frozen human perceptions is warmed by the love of God, new desires arise in our heart and are guided by the divine wisdom. Humankind is drawn into unity with itself. And this inward unity and rejoicing must express itself outwardly; and it does so in material things, in hats and gloves and newly polished shoes, in eager last-minute attempts to get to church on time. As in the sermons of Mark Frank, so here, the unity of inward and outward is complete. The whole method is one of sacramental presentation. Here in the midst of the congregation, the eucharistic assembly of Christmas, the praises of the people are united with those of the angels around the coming together of heaven and earth.

    One of the most striking features of the poem is its use of clanging rhythms and constantly recurring rhyme words to suggest the effect of the change-ringing, at the time a comparatively new practice. The bells become central to the scene. The two poems which stand next after this one in Traherne's manuscript, also have bells as their theme; hard metallic objects, which can yet sound out in the praise of God and summon people to worship him.

      Their iron tongues
      Do utter songs
    And shall our stony hearts make no reply?

Made of the things of earth, of the most base things, yet they can announce heavenly joys to those who hear them.

Doth not each trembling sound I hear
Make all my spirits dance?
Each stroke's a message to my ear
That casts my soul into a trance
Of joy . . .

But bells to ring out clear and true must be whole and un-cracked, and so we must too find unity and integrity.

We must unite
If we delight
Would yield or feel, or any excellence.[6]

Each person, as Traherne at all times likes to insist, since he sums up within himself the whole creation, enjoys this celebration whole and entire. All things are ours, not just collectively, but in some more mysterious way, personally. This is part of what it means that each one is made in the image of God; that each human person is unique, and each a created fullness. And as all things come together into God, so all the steeples with their clashing bells unite in one, and call the people together into God's service. The whole city, the complex articulation of our social life, becomes an icon of the praise of God, a reflection of his glory.

Traherne's poetry, even at its best, does not often arrive at the same quality of ecstasy as is to be found in the finest of his prose. But it is noteworthy that this poem which celebrates the feast of Christ's nativity recapitulates themes and images which come in one of the most dazzling of the *Meditations*, the third chapter of the third *Century*.

It is not always noticed that this vision, unlike that of Words-worth or Edwin Muir, is a vision of the city as well as of the countryside. Indeed it is a vision of the city before it is a vision of the countryside. 'The city seemed to stand in Eden, or to be built in heaven. The streets were mine, the temple was mine, the people were mine, their clothes and gold and silver were mine'.[7] Traherne the child is inside the city looking out to the countryside, discovering the trees outside the city gate.

> The dust and stones of the street were as precious as gold. The gates were at first the end of the world. The green trees when I saw them first through one of the gates transported and ravished me; their sweetness and unusual beauty made my heart to leap and almost mad with ecstasy, they were such strange and wonderful things.

This vision of the city at peace with itself with the temple at its heart – was that his own parish church, St Peter's or All Saints, or was it the cathedral itself ? – was to be rudely shattered by the years of the Civil War, years in which Hereford suffered very severely. The violence and disruption of the 1640s must have weighed heavily on Traherne the boy. It is not surprising that at the time of the restoration of the monarchy he was an ardent upholder of the idea of national and ecclesiastical unity, passionately opposed to every tendency which seemed to threaten it.

The initial moment of vision faded, but it would be reaffirmed in adult life, in the context of a faith in the incarnation and redemption. Here again eternity shines through the things of time, and material objects become vehicles of the divine glory. After experience and suffering it is possible, in the strength of the incarnation and redemption, to affirm again, at a greater depth and with a greater compassion, the primal vision of infancy.

All this is latent within the poem on 'Christmas', and it is clear that something very precious has found expression in it. It seems to embody and show forth the significance of the sacred city as it has been seen and known in medieval East and West alike. It forms a late representation of unities which had found embodiment throughout Christendom, in Novgorod or Mistra, in Chartres or Siena, in Canterbury or Hereford. It seems as if, in the seventeenth century when these unities were beginning to fall apart, people had a last and particularly vivid perception of them. Aelred Squire in *Asking the Fathers* remarks on this in connection with one of the royal houses in Copenhagen. The Rosenborg Slot he maintains, 'from many points of view, like much of the art of the incredibly fertile mid-seventeenth century, is almost a physical embodiment of the thought and feeling of an age that was still in vital contact with many of the common insights of the medieval world. These insights are often clearer and easier to grasp for us today in their late-received form than in their older originals.'[8] This is certainly true here, and it sheds light on the special attraction of the seventeenth-century poets for our own day.

Thus Traherne had a vivid apprehension of the meaning of sacred space. Every city may become the image of the heavenly city, the Jerusalem that is above. The holy city may reveal its features in and through the wood and stone, the bricks and mortar of this particular, limited country town. No one who has experienced the nave and choir of Hereford Cathedral as a place of worship can doubt the effect that such a building would have had on a person of Traherne's sensitivity.

No less acute was Traherne's awareness of the meaning of sacred times and seasons. Every day has the potential of being a day of the Lord, every day can become a sign and sacrament of the great day that lasts forever. But some days are set aside specifically to signify this. These are the feasts of the Church's year. Traherne develops this theme at some length in his meditations in *The Church's Year Book*. In them we see again the importance of the Prayer Book calendar feasts and fasts for Traherne, and of the fact that it contains the commemoration of saints as well as the mysteries of Christ. All this round of feast and fast was something which had been outlawed in the days of his childhood and adolescence. He was already twenty-three at the time of the monarchy, which brought with it the restoration of the episcopate and the Book of Common Prayer. It was perhaps for this reason that he, like Mark Frank, had such a special esteem for these things which had been lost and then recovered.

These meditations also give us an example of a kind of prose poem, which Traherne seems particularly to have enjoyed. One of the most striking of these is a reflection on holy days in themselves. 'Why should we not spend some time upon holy days in contemplating the beauty of holy days in themselves?' he asks.

They are the ornaments of time and the beauty of the world,
The days of heaven seen upon earth,
The seasons of melody, joy, and thanksgiving,

The lucid intervals and lights of the year,
The relics of Eden and superadded treasures,
A grateful relaxation from cares and labours,
The very cream and crown of our lives
Wherein we antedate the resurrection of the dead
And come from our shops to our saviour's throne. . .
They are heavenly perspectives wherein we behold the mystery
    of the ages
Spiritual regions wherein we walk in the paths of God,
Marketdays of heaven,
Appointed seasons wherein God keepeth open house. . .
These days are tastes and earnests of our eternal rest
Wherein we enter the temple as the school of Christ
And like angels are adorned with wings
That we might fly unto heaven,
Wherein like brides we are prepared with ornaments
That we might enjoy the bridegroom of our souls in glory.
O my God, they are mysterious opportunities diffusing our
    souls and elevating them to heaven,
Landscapes of glory,
Golden links uniting our souls and all things together.
Apostles, King David and Solomon entertain us,
Saints and Martyrs visit us. . .[9]

In his meditations on the saints' days, Traherne has such a strong
sense of the sacramental quality of the most material objects that
he is not afraid to speak of the value of the relics of the saints.

In a qualified sense, the very bodies of saints are held sacred by
    us and used venerably of us, being gathered to their fathers
    and honourably disposed of into quiet graves.
For they were once temples of the living God
The storehouses of his holy word
The earthen vessels of heavenly treasures
The living conduit-pipes of the Holy Ghost
The members of our Saviour's body
The relics of celestial kings
The seeds of eternity
Whom nature teacheth us to handle with respect

As we see in the very heathen, who scarce knew the immortality of the soul yet thought it very dreadful not to cover the members of the dead, and with sacred reverence deposited their ashes in honourable urns.

Like the other writers of this period with whom we have been concerned, Traherne makes no direct address to the saints, nor does he make any particular petition for those who have died.

They need not our prayers being already happy,
Neither need we invocate them having free access unto the throne
    of grace.
Yet we reverence and commemorate them,
We praise God for them,
We contemplate their lives,
We imitate their virtues,
We glory in their crowns,
We rejoice in the felicity of his chosen.
It is our duty to God,
Our honour to them,
A benefit to ourselves,
A communion of saints with the saints of all ages.
It is a grand novelty and ingratitude to do otherwise.[10]

It is in this context that we are to place Traherne's meditation on the beauties of Mary, for the text which we are about to cite comes in the pages devoted to the feast of All Saints in the *Church's Yearbook*. If in all the saints we see the potential for human beings to become God-bearing, then this is particularly the case with the one who was called to be the mother of the Saviour. In commemorating her we enter into the very heart of the communion of saints. This is so fine a piece of writing that I shall cite it in its entirety.

And first O Lord I praise and magnify thy Name
For the Most Holy Virgin-Mother of God, who is the Highest
    of thy Saints.
The most Glorious of all thy Creatures.
The most Perfect of all thy Works.
The nearest unto Thee, in the Throne of God.
    Whom Thou didst please to make

Daughter of the Eternal Father.
Mother of the Eternal Son.
Spouse of the Eternal Spirit.
Tabernacle of the most Glorious Trinity.
Mother of Jesus.
Mother of the Messias.
Mother of Him who was the Desire of all Nations.
Mother of the Prince of Peace.
Mother of the King of Heaven.
Mother of our Creator.
Mother and Virgin.
Mirror of Humility and Obedience.
Mirror of Wisdom and Devotion.
Mirror of Modesty and Chastity.
Mirror of Sweetness and Resignation.
Mirror of Sanctity.
Mirror of all virtues.
The most Illustrious Light in the Church, Wearing over all her
Beauties the veil of Humility to shine the more resplendently
in thy Eternal Glory.

And yet this Holy Virgin-Mother styled herself but the
Handmaid of the Lord, and falls down with all the Glorious
Hosts of Angels, and with the Armies of Saints, at the foot
of Thy Throne, to worship and Glorify Thee for ever and
ever.

I praise Thee O Lord with all the Powers and faculties of my
Soul; for doing in Her all thy Merciful Works for my sake,
and the Benefit of Mankind. For uttering the Glorious Word:
yea rather Blessed are they that Hear the Word of God,
and Keep it. And for looking round about upon Thy
Disciples and saying, Behold my Mother and my Brethren.
For whosoever shall do the Will of God, the same is my
Brother and my Sister and Mother. Yea for what thou wilt
say, Inasmuch as ye have done it to the least of these, ye
have done in unto me.

The most unworthy of all thy Servants falleth down to worship
Thee for thine own Excellencies; even Thee O Lord, for
thine own perfection, and for all those Glorious Graces,

118

given and imparted to this Holy Virgin, and to all thy
Saints.[11]

In the article in which he first published this text, J.E. Barnes
discussed the question of its authorship and purpose. He considered
the possibility that Traherne might have copied it into his book of
meditations from some other source. He looked at the hypothesis
that it might have been intended to be used as a litany, each of the
titles in the first section to have been followed by the words 'pray
for us'.

As to the first point, it would seem to me virtually certain that
the devotion is Traherne's. The style is his, and as we have seen,
the content is completely in harmony with his way of seeing things.
It is true, as Barnes points out, that much of the language has no
exact parallel in seventeenth-century Anglican writing, but a careful
examination of its contents shows that it is substantially in accord
with the tradition which stems from Hooker and Andrewes, which
we have been examining. At least this is so, as long as we resolve
the point of its intended use, by deciding that the devotion was *not*
intended as a litany, and that the various titles of our Lady which it
gives are all governed by the words 'whom thou didst make'. Seen
in this light, and in the context of the other devotions contained in
this section of the manuscript, we can see that the whole text forms
one single act of prayer and praise addressed to God, in which the
thankful commemoration of the Virgin is included.

Read thus, the theological balance of the meditation is remarkable. Traherne begins by praising and magnifying God for the
Blessed Virgin. The words used at once suggest forms of prayer,
which though they did not occur in the English Book of Common
Prayer of 1662, had a certain liturgical authority for Anglicans
from their use in the 1549 Prayer Book, and in John Cosin's
Book of Hours. If in his meditation he is going to go beyond
what is customary in the Church, he chooses to begin with what is
commonly accepted. Traherne, indeed, does at once go on to ascribe
to Mary titles and honours which have never had a place in official
Anglican formularies. But, if the terms of the first lines of Traherne's
text are exceptional and go beyond what we might expect, even in
a writer like Frank, when we come to the series of 'Mother' and
'Mirror' titles, we may be surprised at their discretion. The first

group are all either scriptural or closely related to Scripture; the second insist upon Mary as the mirror of humility and obedience, those specific qualities, for which, as we have seen, she is commended by other seventeenth-century Anglican writers. The very beautiful phrase which occurs in the last line of this section, 'wearing over all her beauties the veil of humility', suggests a reminiscence of Taylor's phrase, 'those graces that walk in a veil and silence', or Frank's description of her humility as 'the grace that graces them all'. It is in her humility that her true greatness is to be found.

Thus having celebrated the greatness of 'this Holy Virgin-Mother', with beautiful and splendid titles, Traherne goes on to say, '*And yet . . .*' reminding himself that Mary's greatness is in her lowliness, and that she is one who, with all angels and saints, falls down in worship before the throne of God. The dialectical movement of thought here is similar to that which we have seen in Mark Frank. He, having spoken of the height of Mary's calling, yet reminds us that her blessedness is always a blessedness 'compatible to the creature'. The following paragraph in Traherne takes up again the initial act of praise, addressed to God and not to Mary, for all that he has done in Mary and above all for the promise that all who hear the word of God and keep it shall have a share in her blessedness. Again the themes which we have seen before are present; the words of the gospel are explicitly recalled, it is made clear that Mary stands as a model for all who believe, 'the most illustrious light *in* the Church'. Finally the writer praises God for what he is in himself, and for all his gifts given to the Blessed Virgin and all the saints, and with them falls silent before the mystery of God in Trinity.

In the light of our investigation of seventeenth-century Mariology, it is difficult not to feel a special joy in the reading of this text. On the one hand, it has an exuberance, a freedom, a directness which is not often found in Anglican writing about Mary, from whatever century it comes. It seems remarkably unanxious, unpolemical. In this sense it can stand beside some of the great classical texts of Marian devotion of East and West alike. On the other hand, it reveals a balance and a judgement which is not always present in devotional writing, whatever its subject. It comes from the pen of a writer who had a special awareness of the presence of God throughout creation and who can therefore see Mary's vocation in its fully cosmic setting. In her all creation rejoices. The hidden potential of all things is revealed. And all this is seen in a moment of adoration when with Mary we fall down in worship before God. The praise of Mary is contained within the greater praise of God, to whom alone all praise is due. Traherne the poet and the visionary is at one with Traherne the theologian.

NOTES

1   For some account of the unpublished works of Traherne, see *Profitable Wonders, Aspects of Thomas Traherne*, by A.M. Allchin, Anne Ridler and Julia Smith (Oxford 1989)
2   A. Leigh Deneef, *Traherne in Dialogue: Heidegger, Lacan and Derrida* (Duke University Press, 1988)
3   Thomas Traherne, *Poems, Centuries and Three Thanksgivings* ed. Anne Ridler (Oxford 1966), p. 177
4   Ibid., pp. 189-191
5   Ibid., pp. 100-3
6   Ibid., pp. 104-5
7   Ibid., p. 264
8   Aelred Squire, *Asking the Fathers* (1973), p. 10
9   *Profitable Wonders*, pp. 29-30
10 Ibid., pp. 30-1
11 *Theology*, vol. lxxiii, no. 606 (December 1970), J.E. Barnes, 'A Caroline Devotion to the Virgin Mary', pp. 535-41

Part Two

The Witness Continued

6

From Ken to Heber

It would be a mistake to suppose that the distinctive theological and spiritual tradition which we have been examining so far came to an end at the close of the seventeenth century. There are signs that its influence continued to be felt throughout the period which followed, until, in the middle of the nineteenth century, the Oxford Movement gave a fresh impetus to the Anglican quest for catholicity. But the change in intellectual and cultural atmosphere which took place towards the end of the seventeenth century, a change represented in science by the early leaders of the Royal Society, in literature by the work of men like Addison and Pope, and in the Church by an Archbishop such as Tillotson, certainly brought with it great changes in the world of theology and spirituality. The old confident assertion of a correspondence between humankind and nature which had marked the earlier seventeenth century could no longer be maintained. The picture of the human person as microcosm no longer carried weight. The former highly metaphorical style of writing and preaching gave way to a plainer, more directly rational form of discourse. The minds of the theologians turned away from the study of the Fathers, which had been so characteristic both of England and of France in the seventeenth century. New and very different ways of approach were adopted.

In the Church of England this change was hastened by the schism of the non-jurors which took place following the revolution of 1689. Among the clergy who refused to take the oath of allegiance to William III were many of the most learned and conscientious of the high-churchmen. Although the non-juring body was never very large it contained for a time distinguished figures whom the established Church could ill afford to lose.

Among them were two very different writers who deserve our attention, Thomas Ken, Bishop of Bath and Wells (1637-1711) and George Hickes, non-juring Bishop of Thetford (1642-1715). They were men of sharply contrasted temperament. Already in his lifetime Ken was respected everywhere as a man of notable holiness of life. His stance was notable eirenic. Having made his protest at the time of the accession of William and Mary he retired into private life. To the dismay of his fellow non-jurors, he made no effort to continue the non-juring line of bishops, and indeed at the end of his life returned to the communion of the Church of England. Ken wrote comparatively little prose. Though widely read he was not a great scholar. His output of verse is considerable, but it must be confessed that his poems do not in general show much literary merit. He has been remembered as a saint rather than as a poet, though two of his hymns, those for morning and evening prayer, 'Awake my soul and with the sun' and 'Glory to thee my God this night', have passed into the common use of English speaking Christians throughout the world.

Much less known are his Marian hymns which provide us with a late but interesting example of the characteristic Anglican piety of their time. Ken is at one with the general Anglican consensus of this period in rejecting any direct invocation of the saints. We have no assurance that they, not being endowed with divine omniscience, can indeed hear our petitions. But that they have a general awareness of our condition, and a sympathy for it, he is convinced. In his hymn for All Saints Day, which is addressed to the departed saints, he declares,

> Though in your bounded sphere
> You cannot single votaries hear,
>   And we in no distress
> To single saints make our address;
>   Yet if, like you, we heed
> The saints' communion in our creed
> We of each other's state have general view
> You pray for us and we give thanks for you.[1]

Ken's principle references to Mary come, not surprisingly, in his hymns for the Christmas season. He sees Mary with her child and pictures her sharing in the radiance which surrounds her son. So in the hymn for the second Sunday after Christmas he writes of the shepherds,

On straw they find him in the manger laid,
Till taken up by the sweet humble maid;
As in her arms the dearest babe reposed
A wreath of heavenly glory both enclosed.[2]

This glory which unites Mary and her child is the light which shines out from their mutual love. Ken delights to meditate on this exchange of love between them. The image which his poem suggests to us is that of the icon of the Virgin of tenderness, *Umilenie* in Russian, *Glykophilousa* in Greek, the icon which shows the mother and child united in a tender embrace. Thus in his hymn for the epiphany he addresses the wise men,

You Mother saw and child,
She sweetly yearned, he brightly smiled;
None of the bless'd above
E'er had such interchange of love.
'Twas heavenly glory which the infant crown'd
Dilating his pure mother to surround.

You saw her sweet amaze,
How her full soul o'erflowed with praise,
And how her eyes she tried
'Twixt heaven and infant to divide,
Who taught her love to heaven the readiest way
On his reflex of fontal Godhead's ray.[3]

In the last, somewhat convoluted couplet, Ken seems to be saying that it is by gazing in the face of the child, which reflects all the glory of God, that Mary herself is able to look into heaven. We shall find a similar thought in Charles Wesley later in the eighteenth century.

As we shall see, Ken does not hesitate to affirm the uniqueness of Mary's calling, nor to ponder at length on the reciprocal relationship between mother and child. Her calling to love and cherish the child

Jesus as he grows up, to form him in his earliest years, is to Ken, meditating on Luke 11:27, a greater calling even than that of bearing him in her womb. Her love draws out his love in response.

> God-man his mother pure revered,
> And with a thousand loves endeared;
>   She formed him in her breast
>   By that more nobly blest,
>   Than while her womb him bore,
> As saint than mother honoured more.[4]

Ken pictures a very calm and contemplative house in Nazareth, reflecting, one suspects, his own retired old age more than any memories of childhood. But it is always a picture in which mother and child are held together in a relationship of love.

> In reading, meditation, praise,
> Prayer, charity she spent her days;
>   Ne'er in the world immersed
>   With her dear Son conversed,
>   His beams to recollect,
> And in love-languors to reflect.[5]

Ken sees her heart as the ark of the covenant, the place where the divine glory reposes. Here 'love and hymn' wait upon the divine majesty. We are to understand the Magnificat not as a solitary outburst of love and thanksgiving. It represents Mary's constant response to the divine initiative, a response which is always deepening and growing. The limitations of Ken's verse cannot altogether hide from us the depth of his meditation.

> Her ardent love her hymn supplied,
> Hymn fuel would for love provide,
>   Alternately both fired,
>   Alternately inspired,
>   Alternately increased,
> Their alternations never ceased.[6]

Ken concludes his hymn with the thought that all the saints, like Mary, are called to form the God-man in their hearts and that when they do so they too have within themselves a source of love which can never fail or grow cold.

Perhaps the most remarkable of these Marian hymns is that set for Epiphany I. Some parts of it in a slightly adapted form have become familiar to Anglican congregations through their inclusion in the *English Hymnal*. In the first part of this poem, Ken recounts the whole legendary story of the birth and childhood of Mary. When he comes to Bethlehem he makes a point of underlining the uniqueness of Mary's relationship with her son, a relationship which none of the other saints possessed, and which makes it fitting to compare her calling with that of Eve as something of universal significance. In this extract the lines which are not incorporated in the *English Hymnal* are printed in italics.

> When she to Bethle'em came that happy morn
> Her virgin-eyes saw God incarnate born.
> How high her raptures then began to swell
> None but her own omniscient son can tell.
> *God-man who deigns to temple in pure hearts*
> *A wondrous love to common saints imparts,*
> *Gives them of heavenly love foretasting sight*
> *To comprehend its length, breadth, and height;*
> *Much greater love to his dear mother showed,*
> *Heaven in sweet deluge on her spirit flowed;*
> As Eve when she her fontal sin reviewed
> Wept for herself and all she should include
> Blessed Mary with man's saviour in embrace
> Joyed for herself and for all human race.
> All saints are by her dear son's influence blessed.
> She kept the very fountain at her breast,
> The son adored and nursed by the sweet maid
> A thousand-fold of love for love repaid;
> *Saints, who of God have beatific view*
> *Such mighty joy peculiar never knew;*
> *They to hymn God as vot'ries are employed*
> *As mother of the God they hymned she joyed.*[7]

In view of the common Anglican insistence at this time that Mary is to be seen in the context of the communion of saints and not in contrast to it, this emphasis on the special character of Mary's role is striking. Mary is uniquely close to her son and this relationship is incomparable. Equally striking, though not without precedent, are the lines with which Ken concludes his poem. These lines have also found their place in the *English Hymnal*, and for many Anglicans form a simple expression of their faith in the presence in heaven of Christ's mother.

Heaven with transcendent joys her entrance graced
Next to his throne her son his mother placed.
And here below now she's of heaven possess'd
All generations are to call her bless'd.

If Thomas Ken was a man of prayer and peace, George Hickes was of a different quality. He was a man with a taste for controversy and conflict. From a poor family in Yorkshire, he gradually made his way in the Church. In 1683 he became Dean of Worcester. Like Ken he refused to take the oath of allegiance to William and Mary and so was deprived of his deanery. He became one of the most active of the non-jurors, travelling to the continent to maintain contact with the exiled monarch. In 1694 he was consecrated Bishop of Thetford. In 1709 he became the acknowledged leader of the non-juring community, and in 1713 assured the continuation of their episcopate by himself consecrating three more bishops with the assistance of two bishops from the Episcopal Church in Scotland. But Hickes was not only an active ecclesiastical politician, he was also a man of real scholarship. His pioneering work on the language and literature of the Anglo-Saxon and Scandinavian peoples, *Linguarum Veterum Septentrionalium Thesaurus*, was still in use in the first part of the nineteenth century.

His contribution to our understanding of the Anglican view of the place of Mary is made in a pamphlet published in 1686, when he was Dean of Worcester. It was a time when the presence of a Roman Catholic monarch on the throne in the person of James II was forcing the apologists of the Church of England to strengthen their defences in the face of Roman Catholic criticism. The title of the pamphlet, *Speculum Beatae Virginis: A Discourse of the Due Praise and Honour of the Virgin Mary by a True Catholick of the Church of England,* already gives us a taste of his position. He wants to defend a middle way, to recognize the unique position of Mary within the Christian scheme of things but at the same time to distance himself from the cultus of the Virgin as it existed in the Roman Church of his time, a cultus which seemed to him not only excessive but idolatrous.

Roman Catholic apologists argued that, in the end, all that Catholics did in their devotions to Mary and the saints was to ask for their prayers, in the same way in which we may ask for our Christian brothers and sisters, now alive, to pray for us. Hickes in his pamphlet quotes a large number of specimen prayers, hymns and devotions, and queries whether this defence is really true. If we take such prayers literally are thy not doing much more than merely ask Mary to pray for us? Are they not asking her for precisely those gifts and graces which in strict theological honesty we ought to ask from God alone? It is striking that he quotes not only the more extravagant expressions of the counter-reformation piety, verses of the psalms or the *Te Deum,* for instance, where the name of Mary has replaced that of God or Christ, but also much earlier and less extreme examples of Marian prayers and anthems. The whole tradition to him seems unbalanced.

But it is best to let him speak for himself. He begins his discussion of the topic with the question of the nature of the angelic salutation to Mary as we find it in St Luke's gospel. It is, he argues, a form of address and not of devotion, a greeting made in terms which, although solemn, are by no means exceptional. He looks at parallels in the Old Testament, in the case of Noah and Abraham and Moses, for instance, or, among women, in the case of Ruth and Jael and Abigail. Whether we take the translation, 'Thou that art highly favoured,' or 'Thou that art full of grace,' and he is willing to accept either, there is nothing here that removes Mary from the company of all those men and women of faith who in the Old Testament responded to a particular call from God and found favour in his eyes. 'There is nothing so peculiar in the angel's salutation but that he might have said the same to any righteous person.'[9]

But having established this point on the basis of the biblical evidence and argued that we should see Mary as one among the faithful and righteous of Israel, Hickes nonetheless recognizes the uniqueness of her vocation and its implications for the uniqueness of her holiness.

> She that conceived and bare and brought forth the holy child Jesus, the Virgin mother of Emmanuel, of whom the prophet wrote as he was inspired, surely must have been pure as he was pure, and holy as he was holy... Nay, to be chosen for the mother of God was the greatest honour and favour God ever conferred upon any humane creature. None of the special honours and favours that he did to any of the saints before or since are equivalent to the honour of being the mother of God. And therefore we may be sure that God who said, Them that honour me I will honour, would not have done so great an honour to any daughter of Abraham, but to one who best deserved it, to one of the holiest of the daughters of Israel, to the most heavenly minded virgin of the tribe of Judah, and the royal house of David; who had no superior for holiness upon earth.

Indeed he argues, we know from scripture, that she was outstandingly chaste, humble, and faithful.

> But though we read of no other graces in her, yet we may be sure she had all the rest that could render her righteous and acceptable in the sight of God. There must needs have been a noble structure erected upon such a foundation of humility, purity and faith; where these lead up the dance, we may be sure the whole Chore of moral virtues followed after.[10]

Hickes sums up his position in two long paragraphs in which he sets out first the reasons for which we should honour and celebrate the name of Mary in all the churches of the saints, and then the reasons why we should keep this celebration within definite limits, taking care "that we do not honour her too much, in thinking and speaking more highly of her than we ought to think and speak of any humane creature".

> It is our duty who have the benefit of her example, to honour and celebrate her name and commemorate her virtues and set forth her praises... So divine, so righteous a person ought to

be had in everlasting remembrance and blessed among women from generation to generation. We ought not to mention her name without honour, her name which ought to be like precious ointment wheresoever the gospel is preached, and written in the biggest and most conspicuous character in the diptychs of the church.

If the names of other saints are distinguished with miniature, hers ought to shine with gold. Especially if we consider that she, of all the virgin daughters of Israel, had the honour to be chosen by the Holy Trinity for the Mother of God. What shall be done to the woman whom the king of kings delighteth to honour? Certainly if we should hold our peace and refuse to praise her among women, the stones of the church would cry out, *The stones shall cry out of the wall and the beam of the timber shall answer it.* If what the woman did, who poured forth a box of precious ointment upon the head of our saviour was to be spoken of for a memorial of her, wheresoever the Gospel shall be preached throughout the whole world, surely that most blessed virgin, who had the honour to bring forth and breed up the son of God, ought to have a festival and be mentioned with all due reverence and esteem in all the churches of the saints. Wheresoever the Gospel is preached, that which she hath done and suffered for our Lord ought to be spoken of for a memorial of her, from whom he took that very body which was crucified and that precious blood which was shed for the remission of our sins.

But now the other side of the picture emerges.

But ... though we ought to honour her and have honourable thoughts and make honourable mention of her, yet we ought to take care that we do not honour her too much in thinking and speaking more highly of her than we ought to speak of an human creature. Indeed there is a particular respect due unto her, upon the account of her eminent graces, and as she is the Mother of God. .. But then we must not let our respect for her commence into worship, nor romance her into a deity, because it was her lot to be that happy virgin of whom Christ was born. We must not treat her upon the account of her singular relation to Emmanuel, as if she were an infinite majesty, or as

if her graces were indeed divine attributes. . . We ought not to
pay such homage and veneration to her under the character of
the queen, as is only due to the king of heaven. But we must
carefully keep our respect for her person and memory within
due bounds and limits, lest transgressing herein, we should fall
into those unwarrantable excesses and abuses which a great part
of Christendom is too justly chargeable with . . .[11]

The tone of Hickes's pamphlet is by the standards of his time
by no means extreme, and the case which he makes is in many ways
a reasonable one. As so often happens with controversial writing we
feel that the writer has scarcely entered into his opponent's position.
His knowledge of their stance is exterior, mostly taken from books.
He knows their words more than he knows the way in which the
words function in practice. It will be interesting to speculate why
it was that a century and a half later the followers of the Oxford
Movement found themselves being carried further towards the
Roman and Orthodox position, and discovering that they no longer
needed to maintain the restrictions which the seventeenth-century
Anglicans had placed upon themselves. Was it because they faced,
as we do now, denials of the whole mystery of the incarnation of
a depth and power which Hickes and his contemporaries could
hardly have imagined? Is it in this context that they recognized
the need for affirmations of faith as strong and outspoken as the
denials? Is this why it was that they found it permissible and
even necessary not only to speak of Mary, but to speak to her
with a freedom which earlier had seemed excessive and indeed
impermissible? In face of the denial of all that the communion
of saints implies by way of the destruction of the power of death
and the opening up of paths between earth and heaven, time
and eternity, we find the need to reaffirm that communion more
powerfully and more explicitly.

It seems to me probable that it is in this context that the change
in Anglican attitudes needs to be seen. But if the seventeenth-century
theologians were too restrictive in their sense of what might be
permitted, they were surely right in their sense of priorities and
in their determination to see the rôle of Mary and the saints as
the consequence and fulfilment of the one mediatorial work of
Christ and never as a substitute or alternative for it. There seems

to be something balanced and sound in their constant desire to honour Mary and to recognize all that God has done in her, and yet at the same time always to remember her creaturely status, her solidarity with all creation. In this respect the way in which Hickes concludes his tract is fully consonant with the teaching of such of his predecessors as Mark Frank or Thomas Traherne.

> To conclude, let us always mention her with respect, let her name still perfume the air like precious ointment. Let us celebrate her great virtues. Let us keep her festivals as it becomes true sons of the primitive Church of England. Let us imitate her example and thank God for the benefit of it. Let us endeavour as she did to hear the Word of God and keep it, and to do the will of our heavenly father; and then we shall all become κεχαριτωμένοι, high favorites of heaven even the mother and sister and brethren of Christ.[12]

The eighteenth century was not a time in which Marian devotion might be expected to flourish in the Church of England. It was an age in which the dominant tendencies in thought were pushing people, if not towards total scepticism in matters of religion, at least towards a man-centred moralistic view of Christian faith and life which saw Jesus Christ as a good man who had lived long ago and given wise precepts to his followers. Under such influences as these the majority of the old dissenting congregations, Presbyterian and Congregationalist, became Unitarian during this century. Many have thought that the Church of England would have gone in the same way had not the resolutely trinitarian and christocentric nature of its liturgy, enshrined in the *Book of Common Prayer* preserved its sense of tradition.

In this situation it was clear that anyone who wished to preach an actively salvific form of Christianity, centred upon God and God's work in Christ through the Spirit, would need to emphasize with the utmost vigour the central knot of doctrines, the Trinity, incarnation and deification, which we have found at the heart of seventeenth-century Anglicanism. Such indeed was the stance of the two greatest Anglican preachers and teachers of the century, John and Charles Wesley. Both were nurtured in the theology of the seventeenth-century Church of England, and though the strength of their evangelical experience and their willingness to learn from other traditions, Catholic as well as Puritan, led them to enlarge and adapt that position, they never altogether abandoned it. Indeed its central emphases remained with them throughout their lives and are embodied in the sermons of John and still more in the hymns of Charles.

If we turn to such a collection as Charles Wesley's *Hymns for the Nativity of Our Lord* (1745) we find a fully formed Chalcedonian christology used in the proclamation of humankind's whole salvation. Sometimes, indeed, the theology is so explicit and direct that the poetry seems to be lost.

> Didst thou not in person join
> The natures human and divine,
> That God and man might be
> Henceforth inseparably one?
> Haste then and make thy nature known
> Incarnated in me.[13]

The descent of God into humanity is seen as having directly saving consequences. The one incarnation of the Word is to result in God becoming also in some sense incarnate in the believers. By identifying himself wholly with our earthliness at Bethlehem God raises us up from it.

> Come thou who didst my flesh assume
> Now to the abject sinner come
> And in a manger lie.[14]

For if the divine-human exchange involves the humiliation of God, it no less involves the exaltation of humanity. The characteristic Wesleyan teaching that already in this life we are to seek the fullness of divine love in a transforming union of life is eloquently expressed.

> I long thy coming to confess
> The mystic power of godliness
> The life divine to prove:

The fulness of thy love to know
Redeemed from all my sins below
And perfected in love.

O Christ, my hope make known to me
The great, the glorious mystery
The hidden life impart.
Come, thou desire of nations, come
Formed in a spotless Virgin's womb
A pure believing heart.[15]

Here the parallel between the believer and Mary becomes clear
and explicit. As Mary, a pure and spotless virgin conceived Christ
in her womb, so every believer is called to conceive Christ in a
heart which has been cleansed and redeemed from sin. This is
something we are to look for now.

It might be expected that in such a collection of hymns (eighteen
in all) we should find a number which refer explicitly to Mary. In
fact we find only one, and that a hymn which John Wesley dismissed
as sentimental, 'namby-pambical' was his word for it. This seems
to be one of the occasions when John's judgement of his brother's
work was hasty rather than profound, for a careful look at this
hymn (XVI) which follows immediately on the one just cited, will
show that it draws together a number of themes and images which
are central to Charles Wesley's understanding of the incarnation
and which are in themselves deeply traditional.

The first of these is the idea of the union between angelic and
human worlds in praise of the mystery of the incarnation of the
Word. The best known of all the hymns in this collection begins
thus:

Let earth and heaven combine
    Angels and men agree,
To praise in songs divine
    The incarnate Deity,
Our God contracted to a span
    Incomprehensibly made man.[16]

The union of angelic and human praise underlines the cosmic
significance of the incarnation. It is indeed a moment when creation
is made new and the whole creation gives assent to it. This point is

made explicitly in a verse addressed to the angels where the beginning of all things is evoked.

> By him into existence brought
>   Ye sang the all creating Word;
> Ye heard him call our world from nought,
>   Again in honour of your Lord
> Ye morning stars, your hymns employ,
>   And shout ye sons of God for joy.[17]

But this universal quality of the mystery of the incarnation does not exclude its particularity, in this case the particularity of the newborn child. For Charles Wesley this particularly is focused in the child's face. One cannot but wonder if he had not gazed long and attentively into the face of a newly born child, a face over which so many expressions seem to pass. In the verse which immediately precedes the one which has just been quoted his focus is clear. He salutes the human face of God.

> Angels, behold that infant's face,
>   With rapturous awe the Godhead own,
> 'Tis all your heaven on him to gaze
>   And cast your crowns before his throne;
> Though now he on his footstool lies,
>   Ye know he built both earth and skies.[18]

This idea of both angels and human beings gazing into the infant's face occurs more than once in the hymns (e.g., XII.4 and V.3). Indeed in hymn V it introduces the verse which above all celebrates the ineffable quality of the divine love revealed at Bethlehem. This verse is usually omitted in the hymnbooks, but without it something of the power and purpose of the lines which follow is lost.

> See in that infant's face
>   The depths of deity,
> And labour while ye gaze
>   To sound the mystery:
> In vain ye angels gaze no more,
>   But fall and silently adore.

Unsearchable the love
  That hath the saviour brought,
The grace is far above
  Or men or angel's thought;
Suffice for us that God we know
Our God is manifest below.[19]

In the light of these connections between the angelic and human worlds, between the cosmos and the human face we are able to read the one Marian hymn in the collection with proper attention. Certainly it touches human feelings in a way in which the more severely theological hymns fail to do, but it is not therefore deprived of depth of theological reflection. In the first verse of all we may indeed ask whether it is Mary or the believer who speaks or perhaps both.

O mercy divine,
How couldst thou incline,
My God to become such an infant as mine?

What a wonder of grace,
The Ancient of Days
Is found in the likeness of Adam's frail race.

He comes from on high
Who fashioned the sky
And meekly vouchsafes in a manger to lie.

Our God ever blest
With oxen doth rest,
Is nursed by his creature, and hangs at the breast.

So heavenly-mild
His innocence smiled
No wonder the mother should worship the child.

The angels she knew
Had worshipped him too
And still they confess adoration is due.

On Jesus's face
With eager amaze
And pleasure ecstatic the cherubim gaze.

Their newly born king
Transported they sing
And heaven and earth with the triumph doth ring.[20]

As in Thomas Ken's verses so here it is the exchange of love between mother and child which has captured the writer's attention. Mary herself represents humanity in worshipping the newborn king, the angels come in as the frame to the picture. In subsequent verses the shepherds, the wise men, and then the hymn-writer himself arrive to pay their homage.

The shepherds behold
Him promised of old
By angels attended, by prophets foretold.

The wise men adore
And bring him their store,
The rich are permitted to follow the poor.

To the inn they repair
To see the young heir,
The inn is a palace, for Jesus is there.

Who now would be great,
And not rather wait
On Jesus their lord, in his humble estate?

Like him would I be,
My master I see
In a stable; a stable shall satisfy me.

With him I reside;
The manger shall hide
Mine honour; the manger shall bury my pride.

God's humility, God's self-emptying finally succeeds in the exploit of overturning our human estimation of ourselves; our honour and our pride, so important in eighteenth-century life, are buried. The mighty are cast down, the lowly are raised up, the rich are permitted to follow the poor.

With the beginnings of the Romantic movement, however, a feeling for the place of Mary in the Christian scheme of things begins to revive. There are many reasons for his. In part it was due to the revolution in attitudes towards the Middle Ages. Suddenly much that seemed admirable and attractive was discovered in the faith and devotion of centuries which had previously been regarded as simply barbarous. In part it was due to a new respect for woman, and a new interest in the feminine element in human experience. It was also, we may suspect, linked with a new feeling for the unity of humankind with nature. Certainly all these factors were at work in the poetry of William Wordsworth and had their part in producing his remarkable sonnet to our Lady, in which she is addressed as 'our tainted nature's solitary boast'.

Within the Church of England as a whole these tendencies did not have their full effect until after the coming of the Oxford Movement in the 1830s. But already in the first part of the nineteenth-century their influence was being felt, not least in the work of a man like Bishop Reginald Heber, missionary, evangelist and hymn-writer. It is interesting to place his hymn about Mary, written explicitly for use in the liturgy, next to the verses of Thomas Ken which we have already quoted. Between them they might be taken to sum up the whole tradition of pre-Tractarian Anglican devotion to Mary. Indeed in the admirable balance with which Heber holds together the Lord to whom the hymn is addressed with the mother whose blessedness it celebrates, we might see something which could be taken as representative of the Anglican tradition as a whole.

> Virgin-born, we bow before thee,
> Blessed was the womb that bore thee,
> Mary, mother meek and mild
> Blessed was she in her child.
>
> Blessed was the breast that fed thee,
> Blessed was the hand that led thee,
> Blessed was the parent's eye
> That watched thy slumbering infancy.
>
> Blessed she by all creation,
> Who brought forth the world's salvation,
> And blessed they, for ever blest
> Who love thee most and serve thee best.

Virgin-born we bow before thee,
Blessed was the womb that bore thee,
Mary, mother meek and mild,
Blessed was she in her child.[22]

There is something remarkable about this hymn which for all
its apparent simplicity manages to say so much in so small a space.
Who was its author, and how does he come to have such insight?

Heber was a man who might indeed be called a representative
Anglican, if such a being really exists. He was closely associated
with the Evangelicals of his day, at that time by far the most dynamic
element within the Church. Yet he dissociated himself from the
Calvinism of their theology, and explicitly accepted the name of an
Arminian. Like others of his contemporaries he turned his attention
to the writings of the seventeenth-century divines. In Heber's case
this interest led him to produce an edition of the works of Jeremy
Taylor, prefaced by a biography. It is interesting to see some of
the qualities in Taylor which Heber particularly admired. He com-
mends 'the wise, and moderate, and eminently Christian spirit of
Jeremy Taylor . . . and his zeal for the essentials of the Catholic faith;
his abhorrence of unprofitable and vexatious grounds of difference;
his piety, his toleration and his humility'.[23] His discussion of *The
Great Exemplar*, Taylor's Life of Christ, is no less interesting. While
he expresses some surprise at his lack of any critical and historical
sense (the work, he tells us, 'relates with almost the same apparent
faith, the salutation of the angel to the Virgin Mary; the Syriac
prayer attributed to Christ at his baptism by St Philoxenus; and
the prostration of the Egyptian idols when the infant Jesus came
into their country'), he shows no sign of being disturbed by the
exuberance of the Marian passages which we have quoted, and
which certainly were not typical of the piety of his own time.

Like the great majority of Anglicans before the Oxford Movement, Heber was fiercely anti-Roman. Although in traditional
Anglican fashion he has no hesitation in speaking of the Catholic
faith and of the Catholic Church, to which his own Church belongs,
he has no doubt that he is a Protestant. But here again we must not
assume too readily that we know all that this term implies. It is easy
to read back into the past, attitudes which do not belong there. In
Heber's case his Protestantism goes with a very high doctrine of

episcopacy. When at the age of forty he accepted to go to India as the second bishop of Calcutta, he found himself exercising an episcopal ministry far outside the bounds of the established Church. In these circumstances he did not hesitate to appeal to the apostolic authority of his office.

> A bishop, as such, is not the creature of the civil magistrate. His authority existed before the civil power had recognised him; it existed while the civil sword was bared against him, in its fullest cruelty; it is recognised as existing already and independently of the civil power, in those very enactments whereby the civil power controls and regulates its exercise. And whether it is found in a state of depression and discountenance, as in the episcopal Church of Scotland, or in a state of persecution, as in the episcopal Church of Greece, or altogether unconnected with the civil institutions of the land, as in the episcopal Churches of North America and Malayalim, it admits no other, and it can seek no nobler source of its authority than that of 'as my Father has sent me, so send I you . . .'[24]

Here, in this remarkable panorama of episcopal Christendom, which takes in Anglican Churches in Scotland and North America, Syrian Churches in South India, and the Orthodox Church of Greece, we find the convictions of the Oxford Movement about the apostolic character of the bishop's office, clearly stated more than a decade before John Keble preached his Assize sermon. Doubtless in Heber's mind the doctrine did not have the full theological weight which it would acquire for the Tractarians, with their vision of the episcopate as the keystone of the whole sacramental structure of the Church. It is there nonetheless, firm and uncompromising. Heber was prepared to act on these convictions in his dealings with his own clergy, and in his relations with the bishops both of the Syrian Church in South India, and of the Armenian communities in the north of the sub-continent. He had particularly close contact with the latter, inviting their clergy to take part in his ordinations, and receiving one of their deacons as a student at Bishop's College, Calcutta.

That the Oxford Movement would change much in the shape of the Anglican tradition is unquestionable. One of the places where we can see this very clearly is in a change of attitude towards other Churches, and in particular towards Rome. If Heber sought contacts with the Oriental Churches it was in order that they should reform themselves after the Anglican model, rather than the other way about. Less than a generation later, young men would be travelling to France from Oxford and Cambridge in order to discover how to reform the Church of England according to the model which they saw there. The criterion of Christian excellence was for them no longer to be found solely or even principally within the Church of England. Between 1823 and 1845 much would have altered in Anglicanism in a way which could not be reversed. There was a new enthusiasm, not only for the early centuries and the Middle Ages, but also for much of contemporary Roman Catholicism. In all these different places, Marian devotion was to be found.

But the passages which we have quoted from Heber suggest that not all was innovation. The commonly held view that the Oxford Movement marks a complete break in Anglican tradition, whether for good or ill, needs to be revised. More often than not it was giving new expression to old convictions, which had been in part forgotten or obscured. Its insistence on the apostolic authority of the episcopate, its feeling of kinship with the ancient Churches of the Christian East, its desire to affirm a degree of reverence for the Mother of the Lord, these were all things which the new movement shared with high-churchmen of an earlier generation. Reginald Heber's hymns express that earlier tradition very well and show that it has a substance which we should not underestimate. It is in different areas that we should look for what is most characteristic of the life and message of the Oxford leaders, in a new attitude to the Catholic Church of the West, a new apprehension of the consequences to be drawn from the doctrine of the incarnation, and a new sense of the sacramental character of all creation. It is to these points that we shall be turning in the next chapter.

NOTES

1 *Bishop Ken's Christian Year, or Hymns and Poems for the Holy Days and Festivals of the Church* (London, 1868), p. 420
2 Ibid., p.52
3 Ibid., pp. 55-6
4 Ibid., p. 101

5   Ibid., p. 102
6   Ibid., p. 103
7   Ibid., pp. 61-2
8   Ibid., p. 64. For a fuller discussion of these hymns see A.M. Allchin, 'Marie et Les Saints dans l'Oeuvre de Thomas Ken' in *La Mère de Jesus et la Communion des Saints dans la Liturgie. Conferences Saint Serge XXXII semaine d'Etudes Liturgiques* (Rome 1986), pp. 17-28
9   George Hickes, *Speculum Beatae Virginis: A Discourse of the Due Praise and Honour of the Virgin Mary, by a True Catholick of the Church of England*, 2nd ed. (London 1686). Hickes was a close friend of Mrs Susannah Hopton of Kington, and is thus associated with the posthumous publication of some of the work of Thomas Traherne. p. 5
10 Ibid., p. 67
11 Ibid., pp. 9-10
12 Ibid., pp. 41-2
13 Charles Wesley, *Hymns for the Nativity of Our Lord. A facsimile of the first edition* (Madison, NJ, 1991), p. 37
14 Ibid.
15 Ibid., p. 39
16 Ibid., p. 13
17 Ibid., p. 33
18 Ibid.
19 Ibid., p. 13
20 Ibid., pp. 39-41
21 Ibid., pp. 41-3
22 *English Hymnal*, no. 640
23 *The Works of Jeremy Taylor*, ed. Reginald Heber (Oxford 1821), p. viii
24 *The Life of Reginald Heber*, DD, by his widow (1830), vol. ii, p. 163

7

John Keble and B. F. Westcott

The theology of the Oxford Movement, though it has often enough
been described, has not yet been sufficiently studied in depth.
What was it that gave the movement such vitality and strength,
intellectual, spiritual and practical alike? We have already suggested
that however important the questions of the apostolic authority of
the ministry and of the Church's fundamental independence of the
state may have been, there were other concerns which lay nearer to
the heart of the movement. Of these, without question, the most
significant was the renewed sense of the meaning and consequences
of the doctrine of the incarnation. At the centre of their prayer
and life, the leaders of the movement affirmed their faith in the
nearness of God, of God who approaches humankind everywhere
and in everything, yet who has committed himself absolutely to the
flesh and blood of his Church, which is the very Body of Christ. It
was this faith which filled them alike with awe and rejoicing, giving
them both an awareness of the sacramental nature of all creation,
and a sense of the particular fleshly nature of the sacrament of all
sacraments, Christ the incarnate Lord.

In the brief but highly perceptive introduction to his selection of
Tractarian texts, *The Oxford Movement*, Dr Eugene Fairweather
writes: 'The Tractarians saw the Incarnation, the Church and
the sacraments as contiguous and inseparable elements in God's
redemptive economy. For the Tractarians, as for all orthodox
Christians, the heart of Christianity was the story of God's own

saving and self-revealing action, which culminated in the hypostatic union of humanity with deity in the person of the mediator. But they did not stop here. To their minds it was no less clearly a part of the Christian message that the saving person and work of the Mediator were effectually "represented" in the Church by means of certain sacramental "extensions of the Incarnation". It was, they insisted, supremely fitting that the life-giving flesh and blood of God's Eternal Son who was made man should be communicated through fleshly signs wrought by human hands. Indeed they were prepared to argue that failure to recognize the "extensions of the Incarnation" stemmed from a feeble apprehension of the twofold truth of the Incarnation itself – on the one hand, that man's salvation comes from God alone; on the other, that God's saving action really penetrates and transforms man's world and man's life.'[1]

On the one hand the Reformation insistence on the priority of God's action was maintained; on the other the materiality of that action in the sacraments, 'transforming man's world and man's life' was asserted in a way which seemed shocking to the religious mind of the England of that day. Pusey in his lectures on 'Types and Prophecies', given in 1836, and, though never published, a primary source for understanding the theology of the movement in its formative stages, writes,

> The whole system of religion, contemplative and practical, is one of God's condescension; God cometh down to us, not we mount up to God. Its corner-stone and characteristic is 'God manifest in the flesh', and with this, as God has appointed it, all is in keeping. Neither the letter without the Spirit, nor yet the Spirit without the letter – prayers, which God cometh into the midst of us to hear; earthly Sacraments, yet full of Heaven; earthly words yet full of the Word, *Logoi*, proceeding from and setting forth the *Logos*.[2]

Here already we see many of the themes of the seventeenth-century theologians coming into view again, in particular that sense of the redemption of the body, in which it will be natural to speak about the place of Mary in the whole scheme of salvation.

In seeking to reaffirm the coinherence of humanity and nature, to see the natural world no less than our personal experience as the field of the divine activity, the Tractarians were of course involved in very great difficulties. The intellectual atmosphere of their time hardly supported them in their endeavour. However, they were able to find at least some allies. They were deeply aware of their indebtedness to Wordsworth, with his vision of the sacramental character of the natural world; both Keble and Pusey speak of this explicitly. Partly through his assistance, it was possible to see the sacraments of the Church not in isolation but set against the background of a universe, sacramental at every point. There were theological implications in his writing which Wordsworth himself had hardly seen. There was also the pervasive if ill-defined influence of Coleridge whose ideas were 'in the air', so that even those who had not read him seem unable to have wholly escaped their influence.[3]

In his lectures on 'Types and Prophecies', Pusey attempts to see the typical and prophetic character of the Scriptures not only in relation to the sacramental order of the Church, but also in relation to a sacramental understanding of the universe as a whole, and to the whole of human history. He quotes Hooker, whose writings had suddenly become relevant and alive again; all things are partakers of God in that 'God hath his influence into the very essence of all things, without which influence of Deity supporting them their utter annihilation could not choose but follow'. He goes on to refer to Wordsworth and Keble as writers whose works exhibit the power of God at work in nature, and he quotes four curiously undistinguished lines from 'The Christian Year' which seem to have been adopted by the Tractarians (Newman also quotes them) as a kind of slogan to express their conviction that to those with eyes to see, everything proclaims the glory of God.

> Every leaf in every nook
> Every wave in every brook
> Chanting with a solemn voice
> Mind us of our better choice.

But not only this; he further suggests that while the sacred history of the Old Testament points explicitly towards Christ,

there is at least an implicit acknowledgement of him throughout the whole of human history.

This inherent significance of images receives its full direction
and completeness in God's revelation. In heathenism and in the
natural world they are significant but not of necessity prophetic.
They express truth, but give no earnest that it shall be realized,
unless indeed in so far as we may

See in heaven and earth
In all fair things around
Strong yearnings for a blest new birth
With sinless glories crowned,

and in some way the very existence of imperfect good does
prophesy of its completion somewhere. Thus the heathen history
is instructive, not prophetic, or prophetic in a general way and
in broad outlines, of the course of that natural providence of
God whereof it testifies and whereby it was produced.

The seventeenth-century attempts to see all things in the light of
God's activity in creation and redemption is taken up and reaffirmed
in a new and less congenial climate. In the theology of the early
Tractarians there was to be no retreat from the external world into
an inner world of piety alone. Human life is lived in the flesh, and
the whole manner of God's activity demands that inner and outer
concur in one. The sacramental principle which extends to the whole
creation, demands no less than this. All is centred in one focal point,
the incarnation of the Word of God; yet this mysterious act flows
out and has its effects everywhere. Furthermore, the divine grace
which descends into the world does so in order that the whole
creation may be lifted up, made new, brought into the Kingdom
of heaven. Humankind is to be raised up into communion of life
with God, a restoration of unity which will be no less than the
marriage of heaven and earth.

In a note on a poem on the marriage at Cana in Galilee, Keble
writes:

The change of water into wine was believed by the ancients to
typify the change which St Paul in particular so earnestly dwells

on: 'Old things are become new.' And St John, 'He that sitteth on the Throne saith, Behold I make all things new.' Accordingly St Cyprian applies the first miracle to the admission of the Gentiles into the Church (Ep. 63, ed. Fell). And St Augustine to the Evangelical interpretation of the Old Testament (in John, Tract 8). And St Cyril of Alexandria (in Cor.) to the Spirit superseding the letter. This then being the beginning of miracles, a kind of pattern of the rest, showed how Christ's glory was to be revealed in the effects of His Sacramental Touch; whether immediately, as when He touched the leper and healed him, or through the hem of His garment, or by the Saints, His living members according to His Promise, 'the works that I do ye shall do also; and greater works than these shall ye do, because I go unto My Father.' Thus according to the Scriptures, the Sacramental Touch of the Church is the Touch of Christ, and her system is '*deifica disciplina*', a rule which, in some sense, makes men gods, and the human divine; and all this depends on the verity of the Incarnation, therefore His Mother is especially instrumental in it; besides being, as nearest to Him, the most glorious instance of it. 'The Mother of Jesus is there, and both Jesus and His disciples are called' (He as the Bridegroom and Author of the whole mystery, they as ministers, servants and instruments) – to this mysterious 'marriage' or Communion of Saints.[4]

In this vision of the faith, Mary's position has again become central. Not that she is herself the author of salvation, but the one in whom and through whom we come to know the mystery of the Word made flesh. Not herself, as Mark Frank would say, the object of our worship, but the place where that object is to be found; 'especially instrumental' in the work of our salvation. And because that instrumentality is in no way mechanical or automatic, but entirely dependent on her own free and personal decision, she is as nearest to him, the most glorious instance of that work of restoration, the first of saints, the Queen of heaven. Furthermore, in this vision of things as Keble expounds it, the doctrine of our deification by God's grace, clearly present in the seventeenth century, but more and more obscured in the following period, has made its reappearance. For it is only in the context of this doctrine that the whole development of devotion to Mary can make sense. Isolated from this setting, the extravagant praises which the tradition has loved to heap upon her become unbalanced indeed and verge on idolatry. Here in this reaffirmation of the fullness of the doctrine of the incarnation, so wonderfully expressed in what is simply an explanatory note to a poem, we find the root of the whole subsequent development of devotion to Mary within that particular tradition which stems from the things which took place in Oxford in the ten or so years following on 1833.

There was, however, another way in which the figure of Mary acquired a central importance for the Tractarians; through their very specific attitude towards childhood. That there can be something sentimental in this it would be difficult to deny. But it would be still more unperceptive not to see that there is in it something more than sentiment. If the Tractarians devoted a great part of their time to church history, it was not simply because they were antiquarians (though some of them were). Rather they believed that origins were important, for societies and individuals alike, that the past was not something left behind, but that in the communion of saints the past was gathered up so as to be a living reality in the present. In the history of the people of God, in the working out of the mystery of the incarnation itself, time allows for the unfolding of a gift which was already there in principle, given in the beginning.

What was true of the whole people of God was, they believed, true of the life of each one. 'The child is father of the man.' Here again we find a typically romantic interest in the pre-conscious, pre-rational areas of human life and experience. So in his lectures on 'Types and Prophecies', in refuting the dry eighteenth-century way of using the Old Testament texts as so many simple predictions of future events, Pusey says,

> What then appears to me of primary importance as a corrective of this narrow view of prophecy is to have well impressed on the mind the significant character of everything which comes from God. The world is full of types and it were probably true to say everything is a type if we could realize it. The words of a child are constantly typical of the future developed being; they speak greater truth than they themselves (the outward organ of truth) know; they speak it in reference to some particular occasion, but indefinitely; they are aware of something kindred to the whole

truth, and have some glimmering of it, but it they cannot grasp. And yet they who hear it will rightly wonder at it, and they who understand it better than the child itself, will yet confess that they could not have uttered it so simply and so forcibly. Its very indefiniteness adds to its reality, comprehensiveness, energy. It comes not from the child itself, but from a power within it; they are in truth the words of God, in the mouth of the little one, so lately come from its Maker's hand. In like manner, the sayings of the Old Testament, tho' they often have not the distinct outline of truth, which belongs to the development, have in them continually a depth of shade, which impresses the mind in the midst of its indistinctiveness, yet more forcibly, and has more religious awe than would the mere outline, tho' ever so distinct.

The Wordsworthian echoes in this passage are too evident to need comment.

What is said here of the Old Testament could also be applied in some measure to the writings of the Fathers, as contrasted with the strictness of definition which comes in medieval scholasticism. Pusey himself makes the comparison later in these lectures. Clarity is not all. Images speak more powerfully and with greater 'awe' than concepts, however distinct. In speaking of divine realities, images which can be interpreted at many levels and which do not attempt to say everything, are frequently less inadequate than concepts, which can deceive by their very clarity, giving us a feeling of having mastered and comprehended things which we can only truly understand if we are prepared ourselves to be mastered and comprehended by them. In this preference for original statements of truth in all the fullness and indefiniteness of their meaning, we are surely not wrong in seeing at least an indirect influence of Coleridge. Thomas MacFarland, in his immensely erudite study of the religious element in Coleridge's thought, deals at some length with the importance for Coleridge of transcending a purely linear view of growth. He comments, 'We too often think of "development" as a kind of progress up a series of steps, the improvement of one's position by the abandonment of a previous position. Actually the word implies an unwrapping of something already there. Its sister words in German and French suggest the same psychological truth;

Entwicklung implies an unwrapping, *épanouissement*, a flowering from a bud . . . Though the data of the world change for us, and their connexions with our understanding, the eyes looking out from our time-eroded bodies are the lights of a soul that does not change.'[5] In this way of understanding how the past is recapitulated in the present, to which reference was made at the very beginning of this book, the Tractarians would have found something which touched them very nearly, a principle vital for their understanding both of human personality and of church tradition, a way of seeing how through time, time may be transcended into eternity.

We begin now to be aware of some of the factors which lay behind the Tractarian interest in childhood. We are less surprised to find that Keble's second volume of hymns and poems, *Lyra Innocentium*, is composed of meditations on the words and actions of children. We begin to see too why it was natural that the thought of the childhood of Jesus and his relationship to his mother was one which came easily to Keble's mind. *Lyra Innocentium* appeared in 1846, the year after Newman's conversion, and the numerous references to Mary in the book caused some anxiety to Keble's friends. How much greater their anxiety would have been had they known that the most deeply felt of all the Marian poems written for it had been excluded from the collection at the insistence of some of Keble's closest friends, who feared that, at that moment, it would lead to unwelcome controversy. Only later in his life did Keble publish this remarkable piece, 'Mother out of Sight'.

The poem, which is dated to the autumn of 1844, takes its origin from a seemingly trivial incident, involving a small boy, who comes rushing into the room expecting to greet his mother, only to find to his intense disappointment that 'Mother is not here'. The time at which the poem is written is significant. Already by the end of 1844, the shadow of Newman's departure began to be seen. The bishops and the general public were showing themselves universally hostile. The high hopes which had characterized the previous decade, when all seemed to prosper for the Oxford Movement, suddenly looked very insubstantial. It is in this situation that Keble pens these lines of a passionate intensity, whose stress raises his verse on this occasion to a poetic level which it seldom reaches. Yes, he seems to say, Mary may be very little in evidence in the Church of England; the Church herself may seem a cold and distant mother. And yet still

the Church is there, and still Mary is there at its heart, the one who
hears the Word of God and keeps it.

Mother of God! O not in vain
We learned of old thy lowly strain.
Fain in thy shadow would we rest
And kneel with thee, and call thee blest.
With thee would 'magnify the Lord',
And if thou art not here adored
Yet seek we, day by day, the love and fear
Which bring thee, with all Saints, near and more near.

What glory thou above hast now,
By special grace of thy dear Son,
We see not yet, nor dare espy
Thy crowned form with open eye.
Rather beside the manger meek
Thee bending with veiled brow we seek,
Or where the Angel in the thrice-great-Name
Hail'd thee and Jesus to thy bosom came.

Yearly since then with bitterer cry,
Man hath assail'd the Throne on high,
And sin and hate, more fiercely striven
To mar the league 'twixt earth and heaven.
But the dread tie, that pardoning hour,
Made fast in Mary's awful bower,
Hath mightier proved to bind than we to break.
None may that work undo, that Flesh unmake.

Henceforth, whom thousand worlds adore,
He calls thee Mother evermore;
Angel nor Saint His face may see
Apart from what He took of thee.
How may we choose but name thy name
Echoing below their high acclaim
In holy Creeds? Since earthly song and prayer
Must keep faint time to the dread anthem there.

How but in love on thine own days,
Thou blissful one, upon thee gaze?
Nay every day, each suppliant hour

Whene'er we kneel in aisle or bower,
Thy glories we may greet unblamed
Nor shun the lay by seraphs framed,
'Hail Mary, full of grace!' O, welcome sweet,
Which daily in all lands all saints repeat!

Fair greeting, with our matin vows
Paid duly to the enthroned Spouse,
His Church and Bride, here and on high,
Figured in her deep purity,
Who, born of Eve, high mercy won,
To bear and nurse the Eternal Son.
O, awful station, to no seraph given,
On this side touching sin, on the other heaven!

Therefore as kneeling day by day,
We to our Father duteous pray.
So unforbidden may we speak
An Ave to Christ's Mother meek
(As children with 'good morrow' come
To elders in some happy home);
Inviting so the saintly host above
With our unworthiness to pray in love.[6]

The poem, as often happens with Keble, is less easy to interpret than might appear at first sight, or rather, and perhaps purposely, it lends itself to a variety of interpretations. What exactly does the phrase, 'On this side touching sin, on the other heaven', mean? Is it a quiet repudiation of the doctrine of the immaculate conception, not at that time a *de fide* dogma of the Roman Catholic Church, or is it more general in its intent? Do the words, 'and if thou art not here adored', mean 'and though here you are properly not given the worship which is due to God, yet . . .' or 'and even though you are not given that adoring love which is your due, yet . . .'? Does the second verse cast doubt on the doctrine of the assumption, or does it merely say that we should concentrate our thought on Mary's role at Bethlehem? We do not intend here to try to answer these questions. Knowing how easy it is to misinterpret Keble's mind, much more subtly patterned than most commentators allow (the classic example of misunderstanding occurred in Keble's own lifetime over the words declaring that the Lord gives himself in the Eucharist 'not in the hands but in the heart', words which were taken to imply a denial of the real presence, a thing which Keble made it clear he had never intended), we leave such detailed questions for a larger one concerning the whole movement of the stanzas in question.[7]

None of the leaders of the Oxford Movement was more consistently faithful to the post-Reformation tradition of the Church of England than Keble. 'What my father taught me' was his constant point of reference. For him the seventeenth-century tradition was not something to be laboriously unearthed from the past, it was something, which at least in principle, he knew as a living reality which he had received in his own childhood, in observing the faith and practice of the older John Keble. In the first of the stanzas quoted, Keble refers to having learnt from his earliest years, through daily recitation of the Magnificat at Evensong, to pray with Mary and to be aware that she and all the saints were near. But in the fourth and fifth stanzas, he is saying something more than that. He is saying that we can and should contemplate the example of Mary not only on her own feast days, but every day; and that we should not be afraid to address her directly, using ourselves the words of the angel, 'Hail Mary, full of grace' a welcome which 'daily in all lands all saints repeat'.

Keble was well aware that, almost without exception, the seventeenth-century theologians had discountenanced any direct address to the Blessed Virgin or to the saints as liable to lead to dangerous consequences and especially to an equation of the creature with the Creator. To ask God to hear the prayers of the saints on our behalf, as is done in the Canon of the Roman Mass, is one thing, and some of the earlier Anglicans maintained – Richard Field and Herbert Thorndike, for instance – that it is not only permissible but admirable to do so. To ask the saints directly for their intercession is something else. George Herbert had written a poem explicitly on this question, in which he says that he would have gladly turned to Mary for assistance, had he had any warrant from the Lord for doing so. But not having such an authority, he dare not go beyond what Scripture seems to prescribe. And here is Keble asserting that this practice, which nearly all Anglicans since the Reformation had abandoned, is one which has the support of 'all saints in all lands'. He is being, in fact, almost as provocative as W.G. Ward, or those of Newman's younger and more enthusiastic disciples, who were asserting clearly that the norms of catholicity were not to be found in the Church of England at all, but elsewhere in Catholic Christendom.

What had happened to bring about this firm conviction in a man who did not commit himself to changes without careful thought? The factors involved become clear in the third of the stanzas quoted. There may be dangers in an exaggerated cult of Mary and the saints, but they are not very menacing for nineteenth-century Englishmen. On the other hand there are dangers which had already been seen in embryo in the seventeenth century – we recall Mark Frank speaking of 'our Lord being wounded through our Lady's side' – dangers which have now grown to monstrous proportions. There is the possibility of a complete rejection of the religion of the incarnation, a rejection which will sometimes be explicit and total, sometimes more gradual and insidious, beginning with a rejection of those doctrines and practices which, as we have seen, the Tractarians believed to be bound up inseparably with a right faith in God the Word's taking our human nature. In face of these dangers, it is only through an outspoken and explicit acknowledgement of Mary's part in the work of redemption, that we can hope to maintain the true proportions and the fullness of the faith. In face of a wholly changed situation, the reserve of the seventeenth-century Anglicanism no longer has the meaning it once had. It should be abandoned.

The Tractarians were not alone in the nineteenth century in being aware of these dangers and in making this kind of response. All over Europe the same signs could be seen. At least one out-standing voice in the Lutheran world was raised at this time in honour of Mary, in order to safeguard the central truth of the incarnation. This is not the place to cite at length the works of N.F.S. Grundtvig (1783-1872), the Danish churchman, education-alist, preacher and hymn writer, whose activity is so unjustly ig-nored in the English-speaking world. But certainly his hymns and poems contain material vital for any full understanding of the place of Mary in the faith and piety of continental Protestantism.

> *Gud os gav hans Søn til Broder*
> *Jesus Christus Gud og man*
> *Salig prise vi hans Moder*
> *Himlens Brud i Jomfrustand*

God gave us his Son to be our Brother
Jesus Christ, God and Man
So we praise his blessed Mother
The Virgin Bride of heaven.

We may also suppose that it was considerations such as these which were among the factors which prompted the enormous growth of Marian theology and devotion in the Roman Catholic Church at this period. Some elements of this development, particularly its extreme elaboration and refinement of theological speculation, must seem to anyone looking at it from outside that particular tradition (and perhaps to some within it) to be unbalanced and aberrant. Others, such as the proclamation of the two Marian dogmas of 1854 and 1950, raise difficult questions for the relationship between separated Christians; though it would be the general thesis of this book, that they can only be treated fruitfully when placed in a larger and more inclusive context than has often been the case. But the most important, the most challenging and in some ways the most perplexing element in all this development, is one not often mentioned in ecumenical discussions, because not formally an obstacle to Christian unity. I refer to the appearances of our Lady in various places in Western Europe in the last two centuries, and quite specifically to the two main original apparitions in France, at La Salette (1846) and at Lourdes (1858).

Here are events, mysterious indeed in the biblical as well as in the popular sense of that word; events which have influenced and which do influence the lives of millions of people and have become part of the history of Western Catholicism. It is not difficult to raise critical and sceptical questions about these events. It is more difficult for someone who is not living within the direct stream of faith and piety in which they occurred, to assess them positively. What was God doing there? What is God doing now in these places? Is he at work or are we dealing with a deep and perhaps vitally important stirring within the Christian consciousness? Perhaps both these things. The fact that at each time the ones who saw were children and ill educated should only increase our respect for the mysteriousness of what occurred. Something was given at La Salette and Lourdes. Whatever it was, Mélanie and her companion at La Salette, Bernadette at Lourdes did not manufacture it.

At the time when Keble was writing his hymn, none of these events had taken place. The whole climate of opinion in nineteenth-century England hardly allowed Anglicans as a whole to take them seriously when they did. There were exceptions, however, and one at least we should pause to consider.

In 1865, B.F. Westcott went to La Salette with two of his closest friends, J.B. Lightfoot and E.W. Benson. Benson was later to become Archbishop of Canterbury and Lightfoot Bishop of Durham, a position in which Westcott was to follow him. It would be hard to think of more weighty representatives of the nineteenth-century Church of England. Lightfoot and Westcott were among the most respected scholars of their time. In conjunction with F.J.A. Hort they made Cambridge a centre for biblical learning. They took the historical and critical methods of German scholarship and used them not to undermine but to restate the essentials of the Church's faith. Moreover, they combined with their biblical scholarship a profound knowledge of the thought and teaching of the early Church. Westcott's great commentaries on the Fourth Gospel and the Epistle to the Hebrews are full of references to the Fathers. If Lightfoot was the greatest scholar of the three, Westcott was above all a man of prayer and insight. As we shall see the visit to La Salette made a deep impression on him. He was so moved by what he saw there that when he returned home he wrote an account of his visit which he intended to publish. Once again caution prevailed. Questions to do with Mary and Marian apparitions were dangerous for a nineteenth-century scholar to handle. His friends feared that he would be misunderstood. 'The Professor [i.e., J.B. Lightfoot] feared that the publication of the paper might expose the author to the charge of Mariolatry and even prejudice his chance of election to a Divinity Professorship in Cambridge.' The essay was never published, but Westcott had a few copies of it printed, one of which is in the library at Westcott House. So far as I know this is the first time that it has been discussed.[8]

What we have is a small sixteen-page pamphlet entitled simply *La Salette in 1865*. It is a fascinating document, not altogether easy to interpret. While in some respects it is surprisingly positive, it suggests a distinct ambivalence on the part of its author. There seem to be three principle strands in it. One, a clear and sympathetic account of the story of the apparition, and of the faith and devotion which it evoked; secondly, a reflection on the nature of the cult and its apparent novelty, for the most part negative but not entirely so; and thirdly a brief discussion of what if anything corresponds to the phenomenon of La Salette in the life of the Church of England. 'The new religion – and it was nothing less as we saw it – must answer to some doctrine neglected in our own teaching.'

Westcott begins his account with a reference to Lecky's *A History of Rationalism* and its assertion that 'belief in miracles has died out in the civilized world'. He points out that this may be true as far as certain kinds of scientifically trained minds may be concerned.

But popular instinct asserts itself in the face of this materialism by the strangest credulity. So far from the belief in the miraculous having died out in the middle of the nineteenth century, it would be nearer the truth to say it was never more powerful or more eager for present satisfaction. There is something of a grim irony in the grotesque forms in which the belief is content to array itself. The most extravagant pretender to 'spiritual' power finds adherents; and Mormonism has other aspects than those of cunning and imposture.

If this was true in the mid-nineteenth century it is surely more true at the end of the twentieth. The grim irony of which Westcott speaks is very evident today.

But Westcott goes on to point out that he is not going to discuss the causes of this tendency to belief in miracles. His aim is more descriptive that analytical. 'Instead of touching on the history of the belief, we propose only to notice an episode which is remarkable for its singular beauty and immediate fruitfulness.' These two qualities mark the whole of Westcott's subsequent account of his visit. First, he is struck not only by the beauty of the place but also by the beauty of what he hears and sees there. Secondly, he is impressed by the way in which La Salette proves fruitful in arousing faith.

The story of the vision of La Salette is widely known; but it is so striking in itself that it will bear repetition. On a bright autumn day in 1846 (September the 19th) two very poor peasant children, a boy and a girl, were in charge of some cattle on the mountains above the little village of Ablandins, in the commune of La Salette.

So Westcott begins his account of the original apparition. He tells the story faithfully and without a touch of irony or criticism. Sometimes indeed his account becomes eloquent; describing the radiance surrounding the 'Beautiful Lady' which the children saw, he writes,

As she spoke her tears fell fast but they disappeared like sparks in the halo by which she was surrounded, without reaching the ground. No shadow was cast by her figure, though the sun shone clear behind her. The splendour in which she was encompassed reached even to the children; and Maximin's dog stood silent by him in the presence of the divine stranger.

Westcott goes on to recount the nature of the Beautiful Lady's message; her call to repentance, her denunciation of the people's sins, her warnings about the failure of the crops, 'the failure of the potatoes, the walnuts, and the grapes'. This was the beginning of the potato disease which was to have such lethal effects in Ireland two years later. He points out that she first talked in French but changed into the local dialect when she saw that the children did not fully understand her, only turning back to French at the end when she said finally, 'Well, my children, you will cause this to be published to all my people.' Westcott describes her gradual withdrawal from the children.

First her head disappeared, and then her arms, and then her feet, and there remained only the brightness. Then the brightness itself vanished, and Melanie said to Maximin, 'It is perhaps a great saint.' And the boy replied, 'If we had known that it was a great saint, we would have told her to take us with her.' And he stretched out his hand to grasp as it were some fragment of the brightness; but the brightness was not.

The story is told briefly and economically with a perfect sympathy; it is being told by one of the greatest New Testament scholars of the Church of England in the nineteenth century, one who had given a lifetime to reflecting on the meaning of the gospel narratives, for whom the mystery of the Transfiguration had a particular attraction.

Westcott goes on to tell us what he himself saw when he visited La Salette in the August of 1865. 'We are not now concerned with the truth or falsehood of the vision, but with the practical manifestation of a belief in it.' He describes the journey from Grenoble to Corps, the nearest small town, and the difficulty they had in finding transport.

> A special service is organized between Grenoble and Corps during the summer months for the conveyance of pilgrims but all the places were secured for the next day before we applied and we were forced to content ourselves with being packed with the luggage on the top of the regular diligence.

They spent the night at Corps and the next day made the ascent to La Salette being duly impressed as every visitor must be by the magnificence of the mountain scenery. They arrived just in time for the midday meal at the monastery and 'were welcomed at once without question at the table'.

> In the afternoon, after vespers, 'an exposition of the miracle' was given by the side of the sacred spring. The scene was one which could not easily be forgotten. The spring is the centre of the picture. Above this is placed a noble bronze figure representing the Beautiful Lady in the position and on the spot in which she was first seen by the children. A few paces lower down is a larger group portraying the conversation. From this a zigzag path – the course of the path is very human, marked by little white crosses – shows the way up the slope by which the lady passed from the children to the point of her ascent, over which a very graceful chapel is placed. The slope opposite the spring, crowned by the chapel, and bordered by the sacred walk, forms a natural amphitheatre and on this the audience group themselves.

Westcott speculates as to what the feeling of the pilgrims might be.

Most of them probably were filled with a strange feeling of awe and expectation in which we could not but share as they waited to listen to the mysterious narrative at the very place which it declared to be holy ground.

He then describes the way in which a priest briefly recounted the story of the apparition, and went on to speak of miracles of healing. Having described one of which he himself was a witness, he appealed to the others present to tell of any known to them.

To our surprise, the leader of the party, whom we had seen at Corps the night before, stepped out ... He proved to be Dr H-, a physician from the neighbourhood of Nantes and there was nothing in his appearance which could suggest the least suspicion of credulity or enthusiasm.

So he tells his story; and then others tell theirs.

One narrative followed another. It would be easy to raise doubts as to the supernatural character of any of the cures which were related; but the faith to which they bore witness was genuine and vigorous.

Westcott was particularly struck by the attitude of one peasant who had come with a bottle to collect holy water from the spring. 'If simple trust could bring relief to a sufferer it was impossible not to hope that the draught which he afterwards bore home would cheer the sickbed which he had left.'

The next day Westcott heard an account of a cure which particularly impressed him, this time told by a 'family of considerable distinction in Marseilles' who had come to give thanks for the healing of their daughter. Again he recounts the story as he heard it and comments,

A written narrative can convey no notion of the effect of such a recital. The eager energy of the father, the modest thankfulness of the daughter, the quick glances of the spectators from one to another, the calm satisfaction of the priest, the comments of look and nod, combined to form a scene which appeared hardly to belong to the nineteenth century. An age of faith was restored before us to its ancient guise.

And now Westcott allows himself a first comment on what he has seen.

We talked about the cures to a young layman who had shown us throughout singular courtesy. When we remarked upon the peculiar circumstances by which they were attended, his own comment was: *'Sans croire, comment l'expliquer?'* and in this lay the real significance and power of the place. It gave expression to an instinct which claims to be recognized. It is perhaps not too much to say that the vitality of a religion may be measured by the intensity of the belief in the immediate working of a divine power which it produces. This is not the place for a theological discussion, but a very little reflection will show that when the belief in the miraculous – in the action of a special providence as it is called – as an element in common life is destroyed, religion is destroyed at the same time, so far as religion includes the ideas of worship and prayer.

Up till now Westcott's account has been entirely positive. He tells us what he has heard and seen and he does not disguise the fact that he has been moved and fascinated by the experience.

Now what is he to make of it? His first comment is that while the religion of La Salette is undoubtedly living, it is also new. It is new both in the sense that the event it celebrates is recent, and also in the contemporary way in which it celebrates it. In words which tell us much about the sensibilities of a nineteenth-century Englishman, he says,

There is nothing like the black image of Le Puy, or Dijon, or Notre Dame de Bon Secours at Rouen, which creates an involuntary sense of repulsion or even of disgust as if we were in the presence of some fetish-worship. The figures of the Virgin which are the object or symbols of devotion are perfect in taste and beauty. They claim to represent simply an historic fact. The very purity in which the popular faith is presented makes its novelty more conspicuously evident.

For Westcott, the essential novelty of the devotion which he has seen lies in the fact that it seemed to him to be entirely Marian.

Elsewhere Mariolatry is an accretion or a development, but here it is the original form of devotion. The worship of the 'Notre Dame de la Salette, réconciliatrice des pécheurs', is the one worship on which, as far as we could judge, all the thoughts of those present were concentrated.

At this point there is much that we would like to know. It seems strange that a man as eirenic and accurate as Westcott should use the term 'Mariolatry'. Surely he cannot mean it in its strict sense? Can he really be saying that he believes those he has seen are in that sense worshipping the Virgin Mary, offering to her the adoration which is due to God alone? Similarly, when he says that all the attention was fixed on Mary, one must wonder whether he and his companions attended Mass on the morning of their second day at La Salette or refrained from attending the Eucharist. Surely there he would have recognized an act of worship addressed to the Father, through the Son, in the power of the Holy Spirit, in which doubtless Mary was commemorated but scarcely worshipped. Here are questions to which Westcott's brief pages give us no answer. One has the impression that he himself experienced a conflict of emotions and, indeed, of lines of thought within himself.

In the brief paragraph with which he concludes, Westcott says that we have something to learn both from the faith of La Salette and even from 'the form of its worship'. 'The vitality of Mariolatry seems to show that it is at least the shadow of some truth . . . [It] must answer to some doctrine neglected in our own teaching.' Westcott says that the question of what this doctrine is may be left to the theologians to determine. He feels the question is one which should occupy their attention.

For till it is solved, we can scarcely hope to make much actual progress in our controversy with Rome. Perhaps too it would be found that the solution would set before us that aspect of truth to which the great masses in our cities would most gladly turn.

The late twentieth-century reader may well feel baffled by this abrupt conclusion. What is the doctrine we are neglecting? Is it the doctrine of the immediacy of God's presence in human affairs? Is it the doctrine of the necessary place of Mary in the mystery of our redemption? Is it the doctrine of the communion of saints across the barriers of death, the sense of the nearness of heaven to earth? Is it perhaps all these things, or is it none of them? We do not know. What does emerge is that for Westcott two things are clear. First, the question raised by La Salette is one which cannot be ignored in our encounter with Rome. Secondly, the understanding of this question might lead us to 'that aspect of truth to which the great masses in our cities would most gladly turn'. Seen from a twentieth-century perspective, both these observations would seem well founded. In the first place, it is clear that this is a matter which Anglican-Roman Catholic dialogue needs to take more seriously. Secondly, the fact that the great Marian pilgrimage places continue to attract large numbers of people from all walks of life suggests that Westcott's intuition was sound. It is noticeable that at Walsingham, the Church of England's own place of Marian devotion, working class parishes are particularly well represented.

We said at the beginning that Westcott's account of his visit to La Salette was a strangely ambivalent document. It is marked at once by attraction and repulsion, perhaps above all by a kind of reverent agnosticism. But maybe it would be better to speak of it as a transitional statement. If it still bears some traces of the polemical position of a George Hickes at the end of the seventeenth century, it might also be said to open the way forward towards a more confident, empirical approach to the phenomena of Marian devotion which has come to characterize many Anglicans in the twentieth century. In particular, since the changes brought about by Vatican II have made it possible for Anglicans and Catholics to pray and work together and to go on pilgrimage together, more and more Anglicans have been following in Westcott's footsteps. They find themselves deeply impressed by the sense of the immediacy of the divine presence and the divine action which is to be found in such places. Whatever the final assessment we give of the original events at La Salette, at Lourdes, or in our own day Medjugorje, there can be little doubt about the reality of their results. These are often impressive and inspiring. In England itself there has been the renewal of the ancient pilgrimage to Walsingham, a holy place with its own story of a Marian apparition, this time in 1061. Here Anglicans have been as active as Roman Catholics in the restoration of the holy place and if before Vatican II the two shrines had little contact with each other, in recent years the situation has notably changed. In France it has been Lourdes rather than La Salette that has attracted Anglican pilgrims; some going alone, some going as members of mixed groups, some in official Anglican parties, often under the leadership of a bishop. All these things would have been totally unthinkable in the nineteenth century, but perhaps we may see them as a natural development of the cautious but eager openness which was shown by Westcott and his friends on their visit to La Salette in 1865.

Meanwhile it is clear that a renewal of devotion to Mary, indeed a new development of that devotion, is something which comes from the very heart of the faith and prayer of the Oxford Movement. It is in John Keble himself, in Newman's judgement 'the true and original author' of the whole movement, that we can see this most distinctly. If in subsequent developments of Anglo-Catholicism, elements of Counter-Reformation devotion were sometimes borrowed uncritically and even artificially, the roots of this recovery of the Church's traditional attitude towards the Mother of the Lord are to be found at the heart of the concerns of the first leaders of this movement which began in the university of Oxford in the decade following 1833.

NOTES

1 *The Oxford Movement*, ed. E.R. Fairweather, p. 11

2 For a fuller account of these lectures, the MS of which is at Pusey House, Oxford, see my article 'The Theological Vision of the Oxford Movement', in *The Rediscovery of Newman*, ed. John Coulson and A.M. Allchin (1966)

3 On this subject see Stephen Prickett's two admirable books, *Coleridge and Wordsworth, The Poetry of Growth* (Cambridge 1970) and *Romanticism and Religion, The Tradition of Coleridge and Wordsworth in the Victorian Church* (Cambridge 1976)

4   Quoted in *The Rediscovery of Newman*
5   T. MacFarland, *Coleridge and the Pantheist Tradition* (Oxford 1969), pp. 161-2
6   John Keble, *Miscellaneous Poems* (Oxford 1870), pp. 256-9
7   Even so perceptive and authoritative a historian as Owen Chadwick shares the widely held underestimation of Keble's original and subtle mind. Cf. the introduction to his anthology *The Mind of the Oxford Movement* (1960)
8   Arthur Westcott, *The Life and Letters of Brooke Foss Westcott*, 2 vols. (London 1903) vol. i, pp. 245-6 I am grateful to the authorities of Westcott House for the possibility of quoting from this document, and to my friend Revd Robert Farmer who drew my attention to it.

Part Three

Voices of the Twentieth Century

8

'*The Ferment of Birth*': Euros Bowen

All the writers whose work we have examined so far have belonged to the Anglican tradition. Euros Bowen, to whom we now turn, is no exception to this. A priest of the Church in Wales, an autonomous province of the Anglican Communion, he stands within the same tradition of prayer and faith as Lancelot Andrewes or John Keble. But as a poet, who handles with consummate skill the literary methods and techniques of classical Welsh verse, he brings to his writing another and older heritage than that of the English. It is too often forgotten that the island of Britain contains not one but two living literary languages, and that the senior of them is Welsh. Despite the fact that the very existence of the language is today in peril, the poetic achievement of twentieth-century Wales – the century of Saunders Lewis and Gwenallt Jones, to mention only two outstanding names – can stand comparison with the earlier centuries of this rich and extraordinarily persistent literary tradition. Moreover, the fact that in Welsh-speaking Wales the poet's craft is still a common pursuit and a common interest, gives to the writer in Welsh a public position and relevance which his English-speaking counterpart does not have. As in Russia, the poet knows that what he says can be of meaning and importance to a great variety of people. His words may be quoted in a political trial, for instance.

It is not only the literary and social position of the Welsh writer which differs from that of the English. His religious heritage is also in some ways significantly different. The history of the Welsh people in the last two centuries has been influenced by the Methodist revival, which began in the first part of the eighteenth century, to a degree which has no parallel in England. The strict Calvinism of the Welsh Methodist movement, in this respect somewhat different from Wesleyan Methodism, and the rejection of the arts which often went with it, have led in our century to a strong reaction. While in some writers this has expressed itself in a desire to reassert pre-Christian cultural values, in others there has been a renewed apprehension of the sacramental character of the Christian vision. One of the striking things about this Christian poetry of twentieth-century Wales is that while its writers have belonged to different denominations – Saunders Lewis, himself the outstanding figure in Welsh letters in our time, became a Roman Catholic. Gwenallt embraced for some years an Anglican Catholicism, Waldo Williams, originally a Baptist, entered the Society of Friends – they have been united by a common vision. All have sought to see God not over against, but in and through, the gifts which he is giving us. In place of the world-rejecting attitudes of Calvinistic Methodism, it has been the purpose of these writers to see the whole world shot through with the divine glory, to find sacraments of the presence of the Lord who took flesh, in the very substance of the world around them.

This sacramental vision has been characteristic of the theological poetry of Wales for more than a thousand years. One can find it in the poems of the *Black Book of Carmarthen*, a manuscript which dates from the twelfth or thirteenth century, but which contains material considerably older than that. One can find it again in some of the work of Dafydd Ap Gwilym in the fourteenth century, the greatest of all Welsh poets. It survives the Reformation and appears again in the work of a man like Edmwnd Prys, scholar, archdeacon and poet at the turn of the seventeenth century. Edmwnd Prys in particular was not unaware of the place of Mary in the Christian scheme of things. In his great ode entitled *On Our Redemption*, the first half consists of an extended meditation on the story of the angel's message brought to Mary and its significance. While it is true that the way of glorifying God in and through his creation was not characteristic of the hymns of the Methodist movement, when a leading Methodist preacher and scholar like Thomas Jones of Denbigh allows himself to write in the style of the fourteenth-century – something he does with great skill – we find the same themes and the same images recurring.[1]

All this tradition has become the inheritance of the Welsh poets of our century, and among them Euros Bowen has a very special place. Coming from a Congregational background, he was confirmed into the Church in Wales during his years as a student, accepting what he himself termed the tradition of classical Christianity. Certainly his whole understanding of the Christian faith and of the world was sacramental through and through. But his poetic style developed in ways which have no exact parallels among his contemporaries. For, as well as being a master of the classical forms, he showed himself a brilliant innovator in poetic techniques. To literary critics in Wales, his work suggested a comparison with the great symbolist poets, French and Russian, of the earlier part of this century.

Euros himself, however, preferred to describe his poetic method as sacramental rather than symbolist. For him it was of vital significance that the sacramental retains its earthly substance. The symbol is not dissolved in the thing symbolized. The bread of the Eucharist signifies and indeed *is* more than bread. But it is in and through the bread that this 'more' becomes present. Everything in this world can become an image, a sacrament of something greater than itself. It is the poet's task to perceive this. But in doing so, the particularity, the specific nature of the created is not destroyed. The theological principle articulated by Lancelot Andrewes is verified in the experience of the poet.

The use of imagery in his poems is thus not thought of by this poet simply as a play of the creative imagination. Rather it is seen as rooted in the very nature of things, in a world which is a world of sacraments and images, where the activity of God is at every stage sacramental. The heart and centre of this sacramental universe is to be found in the incarnation of the Word of God, and the image language of the poet is itself rooted in the image language of the Bible and the Church's liturgy. This language has its own particular structure or logic very different from that of abstract reasoning. At the end of a striking poem on the sacramental Word, the poet asserts that it is precisely through the enactment of the Church's central rite, the breaking of bread, that the word of grace is saved from becoming 'an ideology about Christ', a mere set of ideas and concepts about a long-dead master, rather than the living representation of his personal presence.

In such a vision of things, it is hardly surprising that the figure of

Mary begins to find a place. It is, one might say, a general feature of Welsh writing that it refers rather readily to the figure of Mary and the saints. We may find striking references to our Lady and the saints in the writing both of Saunders Lewis and of Gwenallt, for example.

This is not, perhaps, surprising in the work of Saunders Lewis or Gwenallt. It is more unexpected to find Cynan, a congregationalist minister, addressing a poem of praise and prayer to Ann Griffiths, the eighteenth-century Methodist hymn-writer, in a form modelled on Crashaw's hymn to St Theresa. Waldo Williams, who was brought up as a Baptist and became a Quaker, has a hymn in which he calls on Brynach, the Irish saint of north Pembrokeshire to pray with us and for us in our present distress. Most surprising of all, the Baptist New Testament scholar, John Gwili Jenkins wrote a poem addressed to Mary, in which he recalled the many ways her name had been honoured in Wales in the middle ages, and asked her pardon if in subsequent years she had been honoured less than God desires.

But nowhere do we find so rich a treatment of the Mother of the Lord as in the ode by Euros Bowen called 'Genesis'. It is a treatment which both in its substance and its style has a majesty which demands our attention. As we shall see, the figure of Mary has a vital part to play in the whole pattern of the poem. The subject of the poem, which was entered for the National Eisteddford of 1963, was suggested to the poet by a visit to the new Coventry Cathedral during the summer of the previous year. It is a meditation on the great window, with its abstract design, which is placed behind the font at the west end of the nave of the Church. As H.A. Hodges remarks, 'The writer was struck by the blaze of colour in the window itself, and by the splashes of colour which it throws upon walls and pillars, the polished floor and the unhewn stone of the font. All this is a "ferment" of colour, as he puts it, changing continually as the spectator changes his position, as the sun lowers in the sky and the atmospheric condition changes.' Euros Bowen himself says, 'I saw the window, the central light, the colours all round it and the whole baptistery in a ferment of Genesis. And that is the subject of the ode – the ferment of Genesis in and through the great window at Coventry . . . the genesis of the world, the genesis of Christ, the genesis of the Christian.'[2]

The writer tells us that this being a classical Christian theme, a classical poetic treatment seemed appropriate. This presents problems for the English reader. It is more than usually impossible to convey in translation the quality of the ancient Welsh poetic metres, established already in the early Middle Ages.

With astonishing skill the poet captures something of the style of the 'poets of the princes', the poets who sang in the last two centuries before the fall of the last native prince of Wales in 1282. The lines are full of *cynghanedd*, a device involving assonance, alliteration and internal rhymes. A single rhyme runs throughout the eighty lines of the first canto, and another through most of the lines of the third canto. But this does not concern us here. What is to the point for our purpose is the fact that the theology underlying the poem proves in its own way to be no less classical and precise than its form. It is a theology which has surprising affinities with that of the Eastern Christian tradition.

What is striking from any point of view is that there is throughout the poem an astonishing wealth of constantly changing imagery in a 'ferment' of creation. The poet sees the divine activity of creation in and through the creation of the window. The shifting colours and shapes of the glass become an image of the varied aspects of the changing world of time through which the light of eternity shines. It is a poem full of images of fruitfulness, of peace, of brightness. The movement is slow and majestic, yet full of exuberance and a feeling of growth, for the ferment in the window creates a ferment in the poet's mind.

It is clear that it is the second canto, which speaks of the 'genesis' of Christ, which will most directly concern us. Yet it would be the greatest mistake to isolate it from what goes before and what follows after. The whole poem is a hymn of praise to the activity, the 'ferment' of the Spirit of God, of the uncreated, fruitful light of God, at work alike in creation, in incarnation, and in the birth of the Christian community. The three cantos of the poem, though quite distinct, are linked in a single movement. They form part of one whole.

The first canto celebrates the days of the creation. It reaches a climax in the stanza which tells of the creation of Adam. In the preceding lines the poet speaks of 'a silence whose peace held a ferment of morning', as it were a pause which ushers in Adam's appearance.

He proceeds: 'There in the church on a screen of gladness/I saw an acre between green trees,/And a man there, set apart, royal, blessed,/His hands and their rule in the image of the Desire'.

There are many things to notice in these lines. First, it is said explicitly that this takes place 'in the church' (*yn y llan*). (There is only one other place in the poem where these precise words occur.) At the literal level of meaning this refers only to the fact that the 'screen of gladness', the great many-hued window, is part of the church building. But it is surely not difficult to see a further reference to the vision which is to follow, the vision of man in Eden, in the church of paradise. This is particularly the case because the word *llan*, before it means church, means enclosure, a place set apart. Adam is seen in his royal and priestly dignity, entering into creation as a king and a priest, having rule over the animals and the material order, loving and working 'in the image of the Desire' (*ar ddelw'r Awydd*). In this last phrase we have an interesting example of the theological precision of the writer. In the notes appended to the poem, he speaks of humankind as created (*ar ddelw Duw, ar lun Awydd y Crewr*) 'in the image of God, in the likeness of the Desire of the Creator'. It seems here that there is a reminiscence, conscious or not, of the patristic distinction between the image and the likeness of God in humanity; the image, as it were the static, given character of God impressed upon his creature, the likeness, the dynamic aspect, the character which is in becoming, which is to be worked out as men and women with their hands become rulers and creators with God. The poet himself commented (in a private letter), 'I think of man as endowed on the finite level with creative freedom, God as creative freedom on the infinite level. *Awydd* implies the exercise of freedom.'

This word *awydd* (it is connected etymologically with *avidus*) may also give us pause. It might seem more obvious to speak of God as love, *agape, cariad*. But there are in fact many precedents in the Greek Fathers for speaking of *eros*, the desire of God, which calls out the answering desire in humanity. This is particularly the case in the writings of the fifth-century Syrian writer known as Dionysius the Areopagite, who, in view of the New Testament's constant use of *agape* to speak of the love of God, says somewhat paradoxically that *eros* is more divine than *agape*. The writings of Dionysius have been immensely influential in Christian tradition, and there is something in his vision of the divine activity which can illuminate our understanding of the act of creation as it is celebrated in this poem. 'We must dare to add this as being no less true,' he writes, 'that the Source of all things Himself, in His wonderful and good love for all things, through the excess of His loving goodness, is carried outside Himself, in His providential care for all that is, so enchanted is He in goodness and love and longing. Removed from his position above all and beyond all He descends to be in all according to an ecstatic and transcendental power which is yet inseparable from Himself.'[3] This is a love which is ecstatic in the strict sense of that word, which carries God out from himself into creation, to dwell within the heart of things, so that he who is wholly transcendent becomes wholly present within his creation. It is this free act of divine love which the poet celebrates.

The next two stanzas speak of Adam in his innocence. 'His hope is a summer'; from the earth which he loves 'blameless hours' are his. He knows the light of birth, 'in increasing goodness/In peace and unction: he knows no shame'. In this first canto the fall is not spoken of.

The second canto of the poem is headed with the words 'he came down from heaven and took flesh by the Holy Ghost of the Virgin Mary'. In its course, the image of the garden which has been prepared in the previous lines blossoms out into a whole harvest of imagery of flower and plant. But the poet begins on a note of greater urgency, speaking of 'a ferment of birth, a white-hot ferment/Of fragile colours between strong pillars above the play of the ages'. Here as throughout the poem the primary reference is to the window itself, to the delicate patterning of its colours around the central sunburst, and the massive framework of its stone structure. The cathedral with its great window stands in the midst of the city 'like an ancient peace above the din of the city'. The city's life is itself in ferment, but it is only in the peace of the church that we begin to get glimpses of the pattern which gives meaning to that ferment, which is present within it yet often unperceived or not understood. The movements of human history are seen as a ferment of birth, a continuing genesis. The words *berw y geni*, ferment of birth, at once suggest an association between the Greek *genesis* and the Welsh *geni* (to be born) and its derivatives such as *genedigaeth* (birth). And suddenly in the midst of the ferment a form is discerned, 'like

the brightest of flowers . . . a gentle virgin, like a heaven of snow'.
The first meaning of the image of snow here is that of whiteness
and purity. But maybe in the startling juxtaposition of images of
winter and summer we may see a suggestion of the way in which
the opposites come together when eternity touches time.

There follows a stanza in which a diversity of places and scenes
are invoked to suggest the beauty of the Mother of Christ. 'The robe
on the fair one of the bright childbearing/Is like quiet weather on
Towyn's shore,/Like incense, again, from Dyfed itself,/An evening of
splendour on Ynys Lochlyn,/Fair swirling waters at Aberglaslyn,/Bil-
berries trailing their myrrh on the Berwyns.' Two of the lines (2 and
4) speak of the golden beauty of the seashore at evening and in quiet
weather. Two seem to hint at more distinctly ecclesiastical associations, the incense from Dyfed pointing to the shrine of St David,
the reference to the myrrh on the Berwyns inescapably suggesting a
reference to the great but humble hymn writer of the Berwyns, Ann
Griffiths (1776-1805). Taken together the lines contain a discreet
allusion to the gifts which the Magi brought to the infant Christ and
his Mother, as a tribute from the nations of the world to the coming
of the Messiah. All things are summoned to praise the beauty of the
Creator revealed in the central beauty of the creature.

After a stanza which speaks of the moment of the annunciation,
the poet, having summoned the images of nature, now summons the
images of the scriptural tradition to clothe Mary: splendour of stars,
a crescent moon, the cup of a lily, a rose of light. And in a very
interesting way these images lead us forward into a second group
of four stanzas, which speak of Mary less in herself, more as a figure
of the Church. For the Church itself has its 'hours' of prayer and
praise and silence, 'swiftly fly/The modes of their peace like a rich
conversation'. At such moments of calm, the author comments in
his own notes to the poem, 'the Holy Spirit as bridegroom of the soul
comes into the garden, to the orchard, in a "respite which seems like
a prophecy" of Mary'. All annunciations, all visitations of the Spirit
in the Church come from and point to this central annunciation.
And the poet does not only make use of images from Scripture. In the
stanzas which follow he takes up the images of the Land of Rebirth
and the Cauldron of Birth which occur in Celtic mythology. These
too are fulfilled in this childbearing, and 'every province' of this
land of new life is 'a homage to her'. In her all creation rejoices.

The final stanza of this group of four introduces a new and disturbing note to the imagery, a note which itself points towards what is to follow. We hear of 'the praise to the wine of the divine nature'. In his notes Bowen writes: 'In the orchard, in the vineyard in the church, the Virgin is a cup, a grail for the blood of the Spirit, "wedded to the praise of the Holy Spirit".'

The reference to the 'blood of the Spirit' leads us back to the language of St Paul in I Corinthians 12:13, in which we hear of the Christians drinking of the one Spirit. This is language which was particularly dear to Lancelot Andrewes, speaking to him of the activity of the Holy Spirit in the sacrament of communion and the importance of our sharing in the chalice as well as in the loaf. In Euros Bowen's verses, no less than in Andrewes's sermons, these words point to the eucharist and to the redemptive sacrifice of Christ made present in it. Though redemption is not the major theme of the ode it is clearly referred to in the lines that follow.

From now on the imagery turns from that of the garden and the fruitful land to that of the tree, and in particular the Jesse tree. We have been thinking of Mary as the one in whom the praises of all creation gather. We pass to thinking of her as a topmost branch in the family tree of her own people. We think of the generations of faith and obedience, of struggle and dismay, which lie beyond the simple words of her acceptance of the divine calling. And the thought of the tree, which is primarily here a thought of fruitfulness, carries with it other associations, and we hear of a branch which is a cross which spreads peace abroad. We are confronted at the end of the canto with a sudden very specific image which anchors the whole in a moment of history. It is all 'a ferment' which ends with a Son in a Mother's lap.

We do not need to examine the third canto in the same detail as the first two. It is a slighter and less full exposition of its own great theme, the Holy Spirit coming to the Christian community, creating the community through baptism in which we are born again and become children of God and heirs of the Kingdom of heaven. As the poet says, 'the light/Gives life to us with its rich mystery'. Suffice it to say that as in Lancelot Andrewes, so here our birth by water and the Spirit in the Church is seen as rooted in the birth of the incarnate Christ for us. The font is the womb of the Church. At the end of the poem the fall hinted at earlier is mentioned explicitly, and the ode ends with a quiet prayer: 'May his grace go through us,/Rich to renew us,/A birth within us, and blessed are we.'

It is difficult, if not impossible, to imagine a contemporary poet in England who could handle such a subject with such technical assurance, and such explicitness and exuberance of affirmation. The contrast with the extreme reticence of Eliot in the *Four Quartets*, for instance, is very marked. We suspect that there is something in the position of the poet in Wales, something maybe in the very nature of the Welsh language which makes this miracle possible. Perhaps the very fact that in some ways the Welsh language has been restricted in its use, so that while in poetry and theology it is rich, in other areas it is poor, has something to do with it. But perhaps what strikes us most about the poem, considered theologically, is its extraordinary power to fuse together into a single whole different levels and different moments. As Professor Hodges remarks, 'the subject of the ode is not the window, but genesis as signified in the window. But the two cannot be kept apart. The ferment of colour in the church becomes a ferment of ideas in the poet's mind, and in this again he sees the ferment of the divine activity.' The whole poem operates at many levels and yet all are drawn together into one.

As the poet himself expounds it, the ode is seen as a hymn to the creative, fruitful, healing light which proceeds from the Glory of the Eternal. It is, one might say, a poem about the divine energies, the uncreated grace, the gifts of the Spirit present and at work throughout creation – the light of God seen in the light of noonday and of evening as it shines through the changing colours of the window. It is a paean of praise to the divine Sophia, the wisdom and power of God at work in a ferment of birth throughout human history.

How far the Eastern Orthodox affinities of the poem were derived from a direct knowledge of Orthodox theology is not clear. Certainly the poet had studied the Greek Fathers of the first centuries. He published a Welsh translation of St Athanasius' *On the Incarnation*. But I incline to think that it was his knowledge of the classical world of Greece and Rome which contributed most to his sense of the all-encompassing activity of the wisdom of God. This was an activity which he saw vividly in the natural world and in the course of human history as well as in the central strands of God's revelation of himself in Christ. He was after all a learned poet, the translator of a number of Sophocles' plays, as well as of the Georgics of Virgil. Early Celtic Christianity had it in common with the early Christian centuries in the Graeco-Latin world that it was conscious of the resources of divine grace in the world outside the realm of Israel old and new. This did not imply a total acceptance of the pre-Christian heritage. The early Christian writers saw it as something in which error and darkness were always mixed, and some were more pessimistic in their attitude than others. Euros certainly stood on the affirmative side and all this early Christian heritage, both classical and Celtic, had its part in shaping the theological presuppositions of his poetry and giving it its particularly Sophianic quality.

What is clear is that for him this wisdom contains a principle of unity within itself which does not imply uniformity – a unity which is rooted in the particular, transforming but not obliterating it. Mary stands as the personification of the rooted, the singular, she who had her dwelling among her own people. It is in her that the unifying glory of the divine is made manifest. If we were to mention a twentieth-century theologian whose writing it suggests to us, we should incline rather to Bulgakov than to Barth or to Brunner. It is a poem which reaffirms the doctrine of humankind's creation in the image and likeness of its Maker, and which sees the work of incarnation and redemption as itself completed in a further coming, the coming of the Spirit in the Church. In such a vision it is not surprising that 'the fair one of the bright childbearing' should hold a central place, she to whom 'every province' of the Spirit's Kingdom pays homage. What may surprise us is the quiet assurance with which the poet sings the beauty of her humility. It is, moreover, he himself who has brought her into the centre of the picture, for while the font itself speaks of rebirth in baptism, and the window images the light of creation, the cathedral baptistery contains no explicit reference to the Blessed Virgin. Only the poet has made the connection, which sees her as the centre or type of the Church, a cup, a grail for the coming of the Spirit, the place where creation has received the fullness of the Godhead.

NOTES

1   A general introduction to this history is to be found in A.M. Allchin, *Praise Above All: Discovering the Welsh Tradition* (Cardiff 1991)

2   The poem is to be found in the volume of poems by Euros
     Bowen entitled *Myfyrion* (Liverpool 1963), pp. 104-11. The
     poem is followed by three pages of notes and comments by
     the author, from which these remarks are taken. I have made
     use of an unpublished translation by the late Professor H.A.
     Hodges, as also of his own most perceptive notes on the poem.
3   Dionysius the Areopagite, *On the Divine Names and The
     Mystical Theology*, trans. C.E. Rolt (London 1951), p. 106.
4   A selection of Euros Bowen's poems in translation has recently
     been published: *Euros Bowen: Priest-Poet*, ed. Cynthia and
     Saunders Davies (Penarth 1993).

9

'The One Annunciation':
Edwin Muir and T.S. Eliot

We have said in an earlier chapter that Christianity involves the meeting of time and eternity. Two 'todays', one temporal and one eternal, are united, fused into one. In the conjuction of apparent opposites the genuinely new comes to birth. God the eternal enters time, humankind in its creatureliness opens itself in an act of free and willing obedience. When this happens, time is fulfilled in being transcended, human life begins to expand into its true and eternal dimensions.

In the twentieth century we live in a civilization which finds it particularly difficult to realize this mystery. Our society carries within itself a great weight of despair, a stifling sense of futility, because for us time seems to have become trapped within its own limiting dimensions. We deeply doubt whether this opening on to eternity is possible at all, or whether it can be more than a comforting illusion. The time sequence runs on inexorably and finds no fulfilment either within or beyond itself. Perhaps even, it is tied down to an iron rule of recurrence, so that everything that has happened once is bound to happen again, over and over again.

This at least was the fear of Edwin Muir, at the time when as a young man he was most strongly influenced by Nietzsche's idea of an eternal return. Throughout the whole of his life Muir was haunted by the mystery of time and eternity. If the intimations of immortality which he experienced so powerfully in his childhood, and which he describes with such vividness in the opening chapter of his *Autobiography*, were not true, if human beings were indeed creatures doomed to live and die in time alone, then he could only see himself and his fellows as a random collection of dressed-up animals. He tells us of a frightening moment of vision when this thought came to him with an overpowering insistence. He wrote in his diary in 1939, 'Once long ago when I was sitting in a crowded tram-car in Glasgow, I was overcome by the feeling that all the people there were animals; a collection of animals all being borne along in a curious contrivance in a huge city where, far and wide, there was not an immortal soul. I did not believe in immortality at the time, and thought I was happy in my unbelief . . . But now I know that if you deny people immortality you deny them humanity.'[1]

This incident took place in his early manhood, when he was suffering the full effect of the shattering series of events which followed his family's move from the Orkneys, where he was born and grew up, into the slums of Edwardian Glasgow. As time went on, and particularly after his marriage, he began to come to himself, to recover his first vision, to discover the deeper meaning of his life and calling. He came to see that the life of humanity in time is constantly touched by moments of eternity, and that these moments in which time and eternity meet are moments of redemption. In and through time, something from beyond time makes itself known and restores to time its meaning and direction. This process of rediscovery was for him a long and occasionally a painful one. But by the early 1940s it was coming to a climax, a climax which is recorded in a collection of poems called *The Narrow Place*, first published in 1943.

We can see this rediscovery in one of the poems in that book in which Muir draws on the matter of Scottish history, picturing the old heroic king Robert Bruce on his deathbed, haunted by the thought of Comyn's murder which had brought him to the throne, haunted by all the killing which had been involved in the necessary defence of his country's freedom. It is only in the cross of Christ that release can come from the endless repetition of such acts:

> But that Christ hung upon the cross
>   Comyn would rot until time's end
> And bury my sin in boundless dust,
>   For there is no amend
>
> In order; yet in order run

> All things in unreturning ways.
> If Christ live not, nothing is there
> For sorrow or for praise.[2]

This sense that in Christ's death there is a source of liberating forgiveness grew stronger in Muir as he grew older. It is expressed more fully in a poem written much later in his life, at a time when he was teaching in Cambridge, Massachusetts. There he speaks of the cross as the place where God and humanity in more than love's embrace together suffer and die, so that a possibility of freedom is given to humankind and 'man will not *die in time, alone*'.[3] One has to have followed Muir's anguished conflict with the fear that human beings might live and die solely in time, to feel the full weight of those last simple but telling words.

In the Christian story, this process which finds its climax in the cross, begins at that moment when eternity greets time, which we call the annunciation. Muir was to write two poems with this title. The first of them follows closely on the poem about Robert Bruce, and it is a very personal poem. For Muir a large part of the possibility of finding a way of liberation had been given through his relationship with his wife, his love for her, her love for him. They were very different people. She had much of the tough, outgoing quality which he, with his intense sensitivity to people and places, lacked. When you went to tea with them, it was she who came forward and did most of the talking, apparently taking the first place. Between them, in their mutual love, something very remarkable was given and received. So in this poem called 'The Annunciation', he speaks of that exchange. The love which is celebrated is their love for one another. Roger Knight, in his valuable and perceptive study of Muir's work, points out that this poem marks a definite turning point in Muir's development. After a long period of struggle and inner conflict something new appears. 'The "Annunciation" is the first poem of unqualified triumph, of escape from that reign (the "iron reign" of time and necessity, determination and death); the anguish, the yearning, the meditations have given way to a simple song, a song of celebration.'[4]

In the collection in which it appears, 'The Annunciation' is immediately followed by two other poems addressed to Willa Muir, which have the same radiantly happy quality: 'The Confirmation' and 'The Commemoration'. All three celebrate the gift of a relationship which time cannot unmake, a relationship in which each calls out in the other unrealized possibilities of good,

> Each awakes in each
> What else could never be.

They speak of the coming together of body and soul in a relationship which is healing and re-creative,

> This is the most
> That soul and body can
> To make us each for each
> And in our spirit whole.[5]

Commenting on these lines, Knight remarks on the simplicity and directness with which Muir speaks in these poems. 'Muir trusts words, trusts them as carriers of what matters to men, and he here calls upon them to give their natural shaping to a natural emotion. "Soul", "grace", "spirit", "pilgrimage": the ancient words are remade with a total absence of self-consciousness, a total faith in their power to express the nature of love between man and woman in an iron reign whose principal feature is that it denies the realities of which those words speak.'[6] Something similar to this trust in old words still shaped by popular tradition can be found in some of the Welsh language poets who were Muir's contemporaries. A particularly fine example would be Waldo Williams, a man like Muir with a kind of natural visionary capacity; he was also like Muir in being a shining man of great and totally unselfconscious integrity. Muir's childhood years in the Orkneys gave him an experience of a pre-industrial world in which popular memories of myth and legend opened up for him linguistic and imaginative resources increasingly difficult to command in the twentieth century.

We are not surprised to learn that it was in the years when these poems were written that Muir had rediscovered the Christian faith which had always been hidden inside him. He tells us in his *Autobiography* how one evening as he was undoing his waistcoat buttons, while getting undressed, he found himself urgently repeating the Lord's Prayer, over and over again, and finding it full of inexhaustible meaning.[7] He was never to align himself with any particular Church. He stands on the edge of all of them, a radiant figure who puts a silent question mark against our pretensions to ecclesiastical exclusivism. Of the reality of his faith, there can be no doubt.

Muir's second poem called 'The Annunciation' dates from a period some years later, when he was for a time Director of the British Council's office in Rome. This was a time of no little importance in the development of his vision of the Christian faith. In his childhood he had grown up in a world in which the old seasonal rhythms of sowing and reaping and the care of animals were still very much alive. He liked to say of himself that he was born in 1750. But he had also grown up in a land which knew the all-pervasive influence of a kind of Christianity so afraid of symbols and images that in the end it seemed to deny the reality of the incarnation altogether.

> The Word made flesh here is made word again,
> A word made word in flourish and arrogant crook,
> See here King Calvin with his iron pen,
> And God three angry letters in a book,
> And there the logical hook
> On which the Mystery is impaled and bent
> Into an ideological instrument.[8]

Euros Bowen, too, had known the influence of that type of religion. For him, as we have seen, the celebration of the Eucharist is itself the great safeguard against all temptations to make 'the Word of grace into an ideology of Christ'. The whole sacramental method of his poetic art is directly related to the central reality of the incarnation, which is made present in the Holy Communion. It is not for nothing that, as we have noticed, among the works from the world of classical Greece and Rome which Bowen translated into Welsh, these should be St Athanasius' treatise *On the Incarnation*. In him the theological connections are conscious and explicit.

Muir's approach is more intuitive. In Italy he could not but be aware of the fact that he was living in a society which had been centred on such sacramental acts. He was surrounded by the monuments of a civilization which had delighted to show forth the incarnation in visible form. 'You feel the gods (including the last and

187

greatest of them) have all been here, and are still present in a sense in the places where once they were. It has brought very palpably to my mind the theme of incarnation, and I feel that probably I shall write a few poems on that high and difficult theme . . .' he wrote in a letter of December 1949.[9] In his *Autobiography* he notes, 'The cities of Tuscany and Umbria . . . looked like new incarnations sprung from the source of inexhaustible felicity, and though they had witnessed violence and crime, they rose above it into their own world and their own light.'[10]

One particular image struck him. It seemed to sum up much of what he was feeling. 'I remember stopping for a long time one day to look at a little plaque in the wall of a house in the Via degli Artisti, representing the annunciation. An angel and a young girl, their bodies inclined towards each other, their knees bent as if they were overcome by love, *'tutto tremante'*, gazed upon each other like Dante's pair; and that representation of a human love so intense that it could not reach further, seemed the perfect earthly symbol of the love that passes understanding.'[11] Muir, who had known so powerfully in his own life the creative, redeeming power of human love, sees in this image of such a relationship the perfect earthly symbol of a love divine, incomprehensible, unbounded.

> See, they have come together, see
> While the destroying minutes flow
> Each reflects the other's face
> Till heaven in hers, and earth in his
> Shine steady there . . .[12]

Time stands still in the moment of the intersection of the timeless with time. Here, as on the cross, we perceive that God and humankind have come together 'in more than love's embrace'.

In the poem Muir describes both the messenger and the one to whom the message is addressed as caught up in 'an increasing rapture'. Knight comments at this point that here the poem departs from the gospel narrative of the annunciation: 'the persuasion of the poem is that the deepening trance is not supernatural; this love is human too.'[13] But Christianity is in no sense bound to the view that what is supernatural and what is natural are mutually exclusive. The central Christian tradition affirms that grace perfects nature and does not destroy it. Certainly this love is portrayed as human; but as Muir himself insists, it is seen as the embodiment of something which is more than human. True, such a depiction of the annunciation would, as Muir remarks, 'have shocked the congregations of the north, would have seemed a sort of blasphemy, perhaps an indecency'. But it need not seem so to a Christian faith which takes the principle of sacrament and image seriously.

The Fathers of the Church affirm that both in creation and redemption God comes out from himself in love. It is this 'mad love' of his (the term is theirs not mine) which leads him for the sake of humankind to give himself in death on the cross. We have seen in the preceding chapter how Dionysius speaks of God's coming out from himself in love and longing for his creation. Such an intensity of love on God's part is clearly hinted at already in the Old Testament, and especially in the prophets and the Psalms. 'The Lord hath chosen Sion to be an habitation for himself; he has longed for her' (Psalm 132). When such words are applied to Mary, the daughter of Sion, the personification of the Holy City, it hardly seems inappropriate to speak of the angel's 'increasing rapture'. Indeed the Eastern Christian tradition, which has spoken more freely of our entering into the life of God and God entering into human life, affirms that as we increase in the knowledge and the love of God, so God's joy in us increases and deepens.

To speak, as Muir does here, of the angel's 'increasing rapture' is only to speak in a bold and figurative way of the depth and intensity of God's love for humankind, which is presupposed in the very thought of divine incarnation. So again when Roger Knight speaks of the poem as being, for better or worse, other than Christian, because 'it perfectly represents Muir's feeling that incarnation is not a possession of the specifically Christian imagination, still less is it limited to *the* incarnation', it seems to me that he is pointing to those very qualities which make the poem so profoundly and triumphantly Christian. It represents a Christianity which knows that the mystery of the incarnation is not the *possession* of the mind or the imagination of Christendom. As F.D. Maurice says, the truth of God is not something which we hold, it is something which holds us. The word of grace is not an ideology of Christ. It also represents a Christianity which knows that the principle of incarnation is not limited to *the* incarnation. It finds its inclusive and not exclusive

189

centre there. 'The Word of God, who is God, wills always and in all things to work the mystery of his embodiment', as Maximus the Confessor declares. This is the Christianity which we have been exploring throughout this book, a Christianity which may rightly call itself catholic. This annunciation proclaims the joy of *all* creation.

How far such thoughts were explicitly in the mind of Edwin Muir is another matter. In his humility he seems at times to have been unaware of how deeply Christian his imagination was. This is certainly the case with the opening sections of his poem called 'The Transfiguration'. It was only after its publication that he discovered that his vision of the world, as transfigured in the presence of Christ, corresponds to one of the major themes of Eastern Christian thought and devotion. What seems clear, however, is that in his poetry Muir received the gift to express in unforgettable ways something of the mystery both of *the* incarnation, and of all incarnation, for a time in which such thoughts do not come easily.

Muir's first poem called 'The Annunciation' was, as we have seen, addressed to his wife. In a later volume, *The Labyrinth* (1949) he addressed two further poems to her, 'Love's Remorse' and 'Love in Time's Despite', in which he expresses more clearly than anywhere else his faith that through fidelity and love we are enabled to share in a reality which is greater than that of time, a reality whose roots are in the realm of the eternal.

> And we who love and love again can dare
> To keep in (time's) despite our summer still
> Which flowered, but shall not wither, at his will.[14]

Here in what is most intimate and personal something sure and lasting is given and received.

If for Edwin Muir the sense of the destructiveness of time could be an overwhelming and insupportable burden, how much more so was this the case with T.S. Eliot. For Eliot, unlike Muir, was entirely a man of our own age. Muir had always at his back the memory of the pre-industrial world of his boyhood, a world in which ballads and legends, folk songs and folk tales were still alive, in which it was still possible to speak directly of the world of men and the gods. 'The Orkney I was born into was a place where there was no great distinction between the ordinary and the fabulous; the lives of living men turned into legend.'[15] In Eliot on the other hand we feel the full force of the darkness of our age. It is one of the things which makes him able to speak so clearly on our behalf.

It is this, of course, which is set out in *The Waste Land*. There above all we see the sense of the futility which besets a time which finds itself unredeemed by anything beyond time.

> A crowd flowed over London Bridge, so many,
> I had not thought death had undone so many.[16]

How was it that for Eliot redemption came? At the personal level, in ways altogether different from those followed by Edwin Muir. But at the level of their understanding of the inner and permanent content of redemption, there is a curious similarity between the two men, all the more striking because of the great differences between them, both as writers and human beings. For Eliot too there is the discovery that here in time eternity makes itself known, the discovery that God has entered into our flesh, into the very substance of human history, taking the initiative and opening the way for humanity to go forward, to rediscover hope, even to be born again. The way of the discovery of faith is always a discovery of hope, a slow and painful process, often tentative and groping. For Eliot the thought of Mary is seldom absent from that process. We find it hinted at more than once in 'Ash Wednesday'. There the Beatrice-like figure who intercedes for the poet is said to 'honour the Virgin in meditation'. Indeed when she is invoked 'Blessed sister, holy mother', she seems almost to merge with her. And the thought of Mary's prayer for us is explicitly evoked in the words from the 'Salve Regina' which occur at the end of section iv.

But it is in his last poetic work, *Four Quartets*, that we find the fullest exploration of this theme of the relation of eternity to time, and the most direct and unambiguous invocation of our Lady. Already in the opening lines of the first of the *Quartets*, 'Burnt Norton', the question of time present and time past in relation to time future has been announced. Already we are presented with the futility and sadness of a time which knows only the dimensions of before and after, and can see no further than that.

> Here is a place of disaffection
> Time before and time after
> In a dim light . . .

And as if to underline the repetitiveness of such an experience of life, the line

> Time before and time after

is itself repeated a few lines further on. Time unredeemed by glimpses of eternity can never be more than

> Ridiculous the waste sad time
> Stretching before and after.[17]

These themes are more fully developed in the third of the series, 'The Dry Salvages'. In this poem the dominant element is water; the sea provides the leading image. In the first section we hear the menacing but ambiguous clamour of the sea bell. It is worth remarking that Samuel Eliot Morison, the distinguished American historian of the sea, who better than most knew the coast of Massachusetts to which this poem constantly refers, insists on the extreme accuracy of Eliot's recall of the different sea sounds described in this passage. We are dealing here not with unrelated fantasy, but with acute observation and with real bodily images.

> The tolling bell
> Measures time not our time, rung by the unhurried
> Ground swell, a time
> Older than the time of chronometers . . .

This time, which is other than ours, is something to which we shall come back. For the moment, however, the tolling bell inevitably suggests death, and so we hear of

> . . . anxious worried women
> Lying awake, calculating the future,
> Trying to unweave, unwind, unravel
> And piece together the past and the future
> Between midnight and dawn, when the past is all deception,
> The future futureless, before the morning watch
> When time stops and time is never ending.

There could hardly be a more perfect description of a time unilluminated by hope, in which the present has been squeezed out of existence by a past which is all deception, and by a future which is futureless, a moment in which time stops, and yet time is never ending. As in many places, so here, Eliot speaks of a universal condition in terms of a particular predicament. Is not our whole civilization, with its deep-rooted anxiety about nuclear warfare and ecological pollution, with its loss of any living sense of tradition, at times caught up in a mood such as this, where the past has become an illusion, the future without issue? It is in such a situation that

> the ground swell, that is and was from the beginning,
> Clangs
> The bell.

There follows one of the most amazing of all Eliot's technical achievements, the sequence of six six-lined stanzas, in which in each stanza the corresponding lines rhyme throughout the passage. As a piece of poetic virtuosity it stands comparison with the eighty lines of monorhymed *cynghanedd* with which Euros Bowen begins his great ode. There is a technical perfection which corresponds to the sureness with which what is said, is said. Here the stanzas express the sadness of a world which knows no redemption, where all things necessarily and inevitably lead towards death. The very rhyme words chosen are eloquent in this regard; for instance, wailing, trailing, failing, or motionless, devotionless, oceanless, or wreckage, breakage, leakage, wastage.

> Where is there an end of it, the soundless wailing
> The silent withering of autumn flowers . . . ?
>
> There is no end, but addition: the trailing
> Consequence of further days and hours,
> While emotion takes to itself the emotionless
> Years of living among the breakage
> Of what was believed in as the most reliable. . .
>
> There is the final addition, the failing
> Pride or resentment at failing powers . . .

The silent listening to the undeniable
Clamour of the bell of the last annunciation.

We have, the poet says, to think of our seamen as 'forever
bailing'. The life of humankind must go on; we cannot all the time
face the certainty of the end. There is in human beings an amazing
resilience, an unsuspected courage. We continue to strive, 'forever
bailing', but it is in 'a drifting boat with a slow leakage'. And in
the end there is only one issue.

There is no end of it, the voiceless wailing,
No end to the withering of withered flowers,
To the movement of pain that is painless and motionless,
To the drift of the sea and the drifting wreckage,
The bone's prayer to Death its God. Only the hardly, barely
    prayable
Prayer of the one Annunciation.[18]

The force with which we receive the sudden and unexpected
denouement, the weight of the last two lines, tells us how much Eliot
wishes us to ponder the meaning of the one annunciation. Here, at a
moment when we had been driven beyond faith and beyond hope,
there appears a way through; here there is a moment which can
change the direction and the significance of all that has gone before,
of all that follows after, the moment in which the proffer of eternity
is met with the fullness of the response of time. In the response of
the one who receives the angelic greeting, all is restored, renewed.

In the context of such a reversal, brought about in the moment
in which eternity, in the person of the angel, comes to greet our
world of time, we can see that the medieval Latin play on the
words *Ave* and *Eva* – the word of the angelic greeting, the name
of our first mother – is something more than a mere play on words.
Eva is the name which signifies life, for in Genesis Eve is called the
mother of all living. But this is life lived towards death; it is this
movement toward death which is reversed by the word of heavenly
greeting, a word which is full of the Spirit, Creator and Life-giver.
This is a greeting which, by bringing into being a new and direct
relationship between humanity and God, conveys eternal life to
humankind. Thus the life towards death, the life which we all
inherit from our ancestors, is changed into a life which through

death opens out into hitherto unsuspected possibilities of life. With such words of love and rescue, the Kingdom of eternity comes out to greet the children of time.

In this context we can see too that the association which the poets of Wales in the Middle Ages liked to make between the words *Ave* and *Awen*, the Welsh word for the poetic muse, which in that tradition is often considered a direct gift of the Holy Spirit, is also something more than fanciful. In his study of the religious significance of the Welsh literary tradition, Professor Bobi Jones argues that the work of the poet in itself involves a kind of incarnation, a making specific, a giving flesh to what is eternal and universal. The poetic image binds together the seen with the unseen, the limited with what is infinite. By his art the writer restores to words their fullness of meaning, can indeed show us that all our words are rooted in the One who is himself the Word, in whom is the fullness of all meaning.[19]

But this power to give birth to the word is always a gift which comes to the poet. He is to receive an annunciation. The poetic word only becomes creative and life-giving in so far as it is inhabited by the Creator Spirit. It can then become a means by which the lives of men and women are liberated into dimensions larger than those of time. The greeting which the poet or the artist conveys to us is one that he must himself have received. As C.G. Jung says, 'Man is never helped in his suffering by what he thinks for himself, but only by revelations of a wisdom greater than his own. It is this which lifts him out of his distress.'[20] A large part of the poet's craft consists in learning how to be receptive and obedient. We have seen how this was the case both for Muir and Eliot, and how it is that through them, it may be so for us. We are not surprised that in both men, despite the very great difference between them, the thought of the one annunciation should become so crucial. In the 'iron reign' of the century in which we live, we may feel a special sense of personal indebtedness to such men whose words of greeting can restore our courage to be, at times when we had lost all courage.

In the section of Eliot's poem which follows we are referred to the greatest of the Hindu scriptures, the Bhagavad Gita; we hear about Krishna and Arjuna on the field of battle. This reference to another religious tradition is full of significance here. The change in human history marked by the one annunciation is of universal import. It works backwards as well as forwards in time. It is by no means confined to Christendom. And what is of particular relevance to the theme of redemption is the teaching of Krishna about the moment of death, 'on whatsoever sphere of being the mind of man may be intent at the time of death – that is the one action (*and the time of death is every moment*) which shall fructify in the lives of others'. We may learn to live fruitfully, allowing the present its proper fullness, if we learn to realize that the time of death is every moment. We are to live each day, each hour as if it were our last, because in fact it is our last. At every moment, whether we like it or not, we have died to some element of life which will never return. Time itself, even though we may measure it with our chronometers, is finally not ours to control. There is a time which is not ours, which belongs to God. This is the time by which ultimately our lives are measured. And for this very reason the possibility is always open that we shall die not into death, but into life, accepting for ourselves the call of the one annunciation. The bell which heralds death may become the bell which announces the message of the angel.

At this point the fourth section intervenes with its serene and simple invocation,

> Lady, whose shrine stands on the promontory,
> Pray for all those who are in ships, those
> Whose business has to do with fish, and
> Those concerned with every lawful traffic
> And those who conduct them.

> Repeat a prayer also on behalf of
> Women who have seen their sons or husbands
> Setting forth, and not returning:
> *Virgine madre, figlia del tuo figlio,*
> Queen of heaven.

> Also pray for those who were in ships, and
> Ended their voyage on the sand, in the sea's lips
> Or in the dark throat which will not reject them
> Or wherever cannot reach them the sound of the sea bell's
> Perpetual angelus.[21]

At first sight, after the anguish which has preceded them, these quiet lines, asking Mary to pray both for the living and the dead, may seem almost prosaic, banal, 'all those who are in ships, those whose business has to do with fish'. Billingsgate, we remember, is also part of the city of London. Suddenly having turned the corner of prayer, having arrived in harbour, everything seems quiet, human, ordinary. This return to normality, this rediscovery of earth, rather than the storming of heaven, is reminiscent of a strangely moving poem of Edwin Muir's, 'The Good Man in Hell'. In it the writer speculates about what would happen if by an error in the celestial bureaucracy, a good man were to be confined in hell. Would he join in the general chorus of recrimination and hatred, or would he even there succeed in retaining hope and faith – even in hell? And if he did, what would happen? The whole structure of hatred and despair would gradually disintegrate.

> One doubt of evil would bring down such a grace
> Open such a gate, all Eden would enter in,
> Hell be a place like any other place,
> And love and hate and life and death begin.[22]

The insidious power of good is enough to undermine the whole contraption of evil. Suddenly life begins again; not heaven, but this world in its complexity, its mixture of good and evil, its space for human freedom. Even one doubt of evil allows the grace of God to enter in, and entering to make all things different. Muir's poem was published in January 1938. One might call it prophetic, so clearly does it foreshadow the reports which have come to us from the hells of Nazi Germany and Soviet Russia, in the works of writers like Alexander Solzhenitsyn, Sinyavsky or Ginsburg, accounts of the power of naked goodness over against the might of organized evil, to restore a dignity and inner freedom to humanity, even in the most extreme circumstances.

So in the poem of Eliot's, to find the possibility of faith, to be able to open a way for the grace of God to enter in, does not in some magic way resolve all problems. It enables us to enter a world in which it becomes possible to believe in, and even to foresee, their resolution.

In this passage, for all its apparent simplicity, there is much that demands further investigation. 'Lady, whose shrine stands on the *promontory*'; Gregory Palamas, the greatest theologian of the later

Middle Ages in the Christian East, speaks of our Lady as being herself the *methorion*, the threshold, the boundary between earth and heaven. John Keble speaks of a position 'on this side touching sin, on the other heaven'. In his commentary on the *Four Quartets*, Harry Blamires remarks of this word that 'it reminds us that the Virgin's place (historic and philosophic) is at the point where the land whose soil is the nourishment and end of life in the flesh, juts out – into the waters, whose nearer waves are the waves of time, but whose further reaches represent the sea of eternity.'[23]

No less significant is the sudden and explicit quotation from Dante: *Virgine madre, figlia del tuo figlio*, Virgin Mother, daughter of thy Son, which brings into the poem the whole wealth of Dante's own vision of Mary, and his understanding of the affirmative way through his love for Beatrice. This direct quotation, it is suggested, 'injects into the poem a concentrated fusion of allusive overtones which oblique and less readily identifiable literary echoes establish only gradually'. The ordinary allusions, which Eliot uses so often correspond to 'the fitful, particular, experiential hints of an eternal intersecting a temporal order'. This kind of direct citation sends us back to 'the decisive archetypal act of divine Incarnation, of which the Virgin Mary is the instrument ... In this movement the figure of the Virgin Mary is before us as the one whose Annunciation is the pattern of all human vocations to self-sacrifice, whose obedient response should be the pattern of all human responses to vocational demands'.[24] By her free response she opens the way towards the fullness of incarnation and redemption. This is the beginning of that work of God's grace which will turn the tolling bell of the first part of the poem into the perpetual angelus with which this section ends. In the annunciation made to Mary, and in her obedient and willing reply, all the mystery of human liberation from frustration and death is foreshadowed and contained.

This truth can be seen in the very form of the devotion called 'the angelus', to which Eliot refers. It is a form of prayer familiar throughout Catholic Christendom and certainly one which must have been often in Eliot's own heart and mind. To announce it the church bell is rung first of all in three groups of three strokes, and then, after a pause, in nine strokes together. The first group of three commemorates the angelic salutation, 'The angel of the Lord brought tidings to Mary and she conceived by the Holy Ghost.' The second group commemorates her response, 'Behold the handmaid of the Lord, be it unto me according to thy word.' The third tells us of the immeasurable consequence, 'The Word was made flesh and dwelt among us.' And each time the believer adds his own salutation which is also a request for prayer, 'Hail Mary, full of grace, the Lord is with thee, blessed art thou among women and blessed is the fruit of thy womb, Jesus. Holy Mary, Mother of God, pray for us sinners now and at the hour of our death.' Then come the nine strokes of the bell which are accompanied by the following prayer, which is, as it happens, the collect for the feast of the Annunciation: 'Grant, O Lord, that as we have known the incarnation of thy Son Jesus Christ, through the message of an angel, so by his cross and passion we may be brought unto the glory of his resurrection.'

In this form of prayer we hold together in one the thought of the birth of the saviour at Bethlehem with the thought of his dying and rising again in Jerusalem, the present moment of the believer's life, now, with the final moment, the hour of his death, which is already latent in that present moment. We bring together the Saviour's birth and dying with our own. The barely prayable prayer of the one annunciation becomes the type of all human acts of faith and obedience in response to the divine initiative, even of that supreme act which Mary's Son is to make at the moment when he offers himself to death, and in doing so overcomes death.

We begin to see why it is that the moment of the annunciation is the moment which makes sense of all other moments. It is a moment which is truly in time, not out of time. It has a whole series of temporal consequences; the embryo begins to stir in the womb. But it is a moment in which eternity has really come, in which God is present and at work. Both the birth and the death of Jesus witness to the depth and immensity of God's love, and to the infinite openness and potential of human life. And just as, in baptism, the death of each one who is baptized is included in Christ's death, in order that the whole process of dying may become dying into life, so also the birth of each one is included in Christ's birth, in order that the whole process of living may be open to the coming of the Spirit, who is Lord and giver of life. Grundtvig expresses this magnificently in a verse in which he says

Each one has his own birthday
For this world's affairs
For struggle and defeat
And ultimately for death.
But for life and peace and joy
Christmas night with the angels' songs
Is the hour of our birth.[25]

It is in this sense that we may rightly think of Mary as the mother of us all; in this sense that Andrewes speaks of the font as the womb of the Church, of one substance with the Virgin's womb, with a power given it by the Spirit of bringing forth sons of God. From his participation in our human nature follows our participation in his divine nature. The life of eternity enters into time, so that the life of time may find its fulfilment in eternity.

Considerations such as these show us that there is a closer relationship between faith in the Virgin birth and faith in the bodily resurrection of Christ than might at first sight appear. Both doctrines affirm the depth of God's love, the extent of his involvement in the human mess, in the very substance of our human history, its reality of flesh and blood. And both doctrines affirm the potential greatness, the infinite openness of that human history. In the reality of flesh and blood, the eternal is made present and made known. It is not surprising that our own society, with its sense of being held in an 'iron reign' of necessity and death, with its particular difficulty in believing that human life can open out into something larger than itself, finds these doctrines difficult to accept. In some sense, however, this has always been the case, for at all times these articles of faith have brought a judgement on our fallen ways of thinking. They are bound to come to our minds first as a cross and only afterwards as a fulfilment.

But it is of fulfilment that both ultimately speak, for while both tell of a mystery given from on high, they also speak of the fulfilment of what is given from below. Neither Christ's conception nor his rising again is an isolated wonder, unrelated to the rest of human history, to the nature of the universe as a whole. 'The truth, which is revealed in them, is at the same time situated at the heart of history, at the basis of creation and at the goal of history.'[26] All stories of strange or miraculous births, and there are many in the legends and mythology of humanity, hint at the potential of a birth from above, at the mystery of each human life as a new creation, a possible point of the intersection of the timeless with time. The point is well made by Alwyn Rees in his book *The Celtic Heritage*.[27] All stories of a return from death, or even perhaps of an inexplicable escape from death, hint at the potential of a fully human death, which would be a death in which our understanding of death was changed rather than our understanding of the one who had died, in which death would be included in something greater than itself. In this sense the death of Socrates and of St Francis, for all their differences, show us something of what such a death might be.

The birth and death of Christ, given from on high, are a full and perfect confirmation of these half-lost human longings. They are at one and the same time a revelation of the mysteriousness of the divine love which goes far beyond anything the mind could have thought or the heart desired, and also a revelation of the mysteriousness of the human calling and destiny. Planted at the heart of humanity's very being there is an openness to what is beyond it.

> These events stand at the apex of supernatural revelation, but at the same time they are events of the complete restoration of nature to its condition and destiny as nature, that is to say, as the place where the Spirit is made manifest unhindered. For this very reason they foreshadow the restoration of the whole of nature to its true being at the end of time, when the Spirit will rejoice in a full and eternal victory . . .[28]

As Les Murray puts it,

> Like any great poem, that of Jesus is inexhaustible, and not all the books in the world could contain a sufficient meditation on it. Meditation would not be enough, anyway; this is meant to be not merely a poem we can appreciate and gain spiritual strength from, but one we can join. By sharing in our tragedy to the full, embodying it all the way to its tragic end and then reassuming his own embodiment beyond it he confirms better hopes even for our bodies, than we had dared to hold on the basis of our health and our dreams alone . . . The way to our true potential, we are shown, lies not through the rationalizations of the forebrain,

which imagines itself bodiless or exploits its embodiment, but through the integration of all the dimensions of our life, each of which is good and holy, with the Divine.[29]

Thus in Christ it is revealed that both at birth and at death, human life can conquer time through time. The moments which in themselves can be and are the perfect symbols of human bondage to time and of our imprisonment in a world of endless recurrence, birth, copulation and death, become the very symbols of our liberation from death, and of the liberation of all creation. This is not only a liberation from the cycle of birth and death, it is a liberation through them by the taking up of time into eternity. She who stands at the entrance to this mystery, the place where the Spirit is made manifest, is indeed the gate of heaven, the joy of all creation.

NOTES

1   P.H. Butter, *Edwin Muir, Man and Poet* (Edinburgh 1966), p. 51
2   Edwin Muir, *Collected Poems* (1960), p. 115
3   Ibid., p. 263
4   Roger Knight, *Edwin Muir, an Introduction to his Work* (1980), p. 120
5   Ibid., p. 117
6   Ibid., p. 121
7   Edwin Muir, *An Autobiography* (1969), p. 246
8   Op. cit., p. 228
9   *Selected Letters of Edwin Muir*, ed. P.H. Butter (1974), p. 154
10   Op. cit., p. 279
11   Ibid., p. 278
12   Op. cit., p. 223
13   Knight, p. 193
14   Op. cit., p. 193
15   Quoted in Knight, p. 10
16   T.S. Eliot, *The Waste Land*
17   'Burnt Norton'
18   'The Dry Salvages'
19   R.M. Jones, *Llen Cymru a Chrefydd* (Abertawe 1978), p. 210 and pp. 53-4
20   Quoted in Knight, p. 100

21 'The Dry Salvages'

22 Op. cit., p. 104

23 Harry Blamires, *Word Unheard: A Guide Through Eliot's 'Four Quartets'* (1969), p. 110

24 Ibid.

25 N.F.S. Grundtvig, *Sang-Vaerk*, vol. i. (Copenhagen 1949), p. 419

26 John D. Zizioulas, 'Vérité et Communion' in *Irenikon* (1977) no. 4, pp. 451-510. Page 484, resuming the thought of Maximus the Confessor.

27 Alwyn Rees and Brinley Rees, *Celtic Heritage* (1961)

28 Maximus the Confessor, *Philosophical and Theological Questions*, vol. i. Introduction and Commentary by Father Staniloae (Athens 1978, in modern Greek), p. 50

29 Les Murray, *The Paperbark Tree*, pp. 268-9

Epilogue

At the beginning of this book we remarked on the way in which what is universal in Christianity is rooted in what is particular, made known in specific times and specific places. This theme has pursued us throughout our inquiry, and it has led us to see Mary as herself the embodiment of this principle, the one in whom the uncontainable is contained. 'Here', as Mark Frank says, 'is the shrine and altar, the glorious Virgin's lap, where the Saviour of the world is laid to be worshipped and adored.'

It is not therefore surprising to find that in Christian history Mary's name has been linked with innumerable holy places. It was one of the complaints of the Reformers. There were so many 'Ladies': our Lady of this and our Lady of that. 'She's a rare one for locality', as David Jones, writer and artist, puts it. This aspect of the mystery of Mary is one on which Pope John Paul II seems to love to dwell, drawing out in his speeches the multiplicity of the places which are linked with her name. In his visit first to Mexico, in 1979, at the shrine of our Lady of Guadalupe he said, 'No less has been your presence in other places, where your children invoke you with tender names, as our Lady of Altagracie, of the Aparecida, of Lujon, and with many other no less affectionate names, not to give an unending list, names by which in each nation and even in each region the peoples of Latin America express their devotion.'[1]

She it is who, by her vocation to be the place of God, and by her fulfilment of that vocation, reveals the true destiny of all places, indeed of all humankind and all creation, which shares in that high calling to become the place of God's inhabitation. This again is why she is called the joy of all creation, because the whole creation finds its possibility of fulfilment in her. If, as we thought in the previous chapter, all moments of time are touched and, as it were, redeemed, by the moment of the one annunciation, so too all the places where people dwell are touched and potentially opened to the divine indwelling by her acceptance of the angelic salutation. The very nature of time and space is illumined and transformed when the divine presence is made known within it.

And because it is seen in her that this world is capable of becoming the place of God, so again it becomes possible to see it as the place of humankind. For it is only when this world is known as God's world that it can become the true dwelling-place of humankind. In her this world reveals its true quality, as the good earth, the land of promise, the place where God's blessing descends in its fullness. When we cease to try to hold on to this world as our own exclusive possession, when we cease to devour it with unmeasured greed, when we acknowledge it as God's gift to us to be held in trust for future generations, then we are able to receive it and rejoice in it, as our rightful inheritance. 'Blessed are the meek, for they shall inherit the earth' (Matt. 5:5). The promise of the second beatitude takes on all its meaning in this context. Behind it lies the assurance of the psalmist, 'those who wait for the Lord shall possess the land ... The meek shall possess the land and enjoy the abundance of peace' (Ps. 37:9, 11). An attitude of contemplative openness and delight before the gifts of God, a recognition of our own creaturely limitations and fragility, above all a certain awe and respect before the mysteries of existence – these are the attitudes which receive the abundance of the divine blessing. Only in the rediscovery of such attitudes, which are symbolized in the person of Mary, and which have been highly valued not only in Christianity but in many of the religious traditions of humankind, shall we begin to find a resolution of the urgent ecological problems which confront us, as a result of our inhuman rapacity and greed.

The good earth which we inherit is above all the good earth of our own bodies. And it it here that we begin to see how it is that the mystery of Mary responds to and hallows the most basic elements of our common human experience. For if man is a journey, woman is a place. It is the mother who creates the home, transforms an anonymous dwelling area into the place where a family can grow and develop, a place which becomes filled with memories and associations, in which the very things that make it up, and not only the people who live there, are known and loved, cared for and remembered. She does this primarily simply by being there, by her bodily presence, and then by the quality of that presence, 'welcoming and forgiving, praying and receiving, obedient and compassionate, confident and joyful'.[2]

The lives of all of us begin in the body of our mother. We are related to that place, that piece of the material world, in a way in which we are related to no other place. For most of us our first experience of food comes in relation to that body. It is there that we learn to eat and are initiated into the community of eating and drinking, which provides so many of the basic structures of all human community. For most of us our first experience of speech is no less intimately, and only slightly less physically, connected with the body of our mother. This is where our insertion into the community of language, of shared speaking and singing, listening and attending has its origins. When we reflect on facts like these in relation to the human development of Jesus, we begin to see more of the hidden reasons for the tradition of devotion to his mother. As Archbishop Donald Coggan says about the way in which Jesus learnt to pray, 'So we watch Mother and Son at prayer, and in doing so we tread on holy ground.'[3]

The implications of all this are numberless. To take a single example from a statement made by the bishops of Poland in May 1978, about the duties of Christians towards their nation and its inheritance, 'One can suppose that the deepest of all foundations of national culture is to be found in the word of the mother which gives birth to the child's first smile. From that moment onwards, he is inserted ever more deeply into the great poem of the language of his nation, which grows stronger in the consciousness of the child, the youth, the adult, the speaker, the writer . . .'[4] Similarly in baptism, in which we receive our Christian name, God's word is spoken to us and draws out our response, bringing us into the great poem of the sacramental action of the universal Church. There we are reborn to new and eternal life. There we find that the natural communities of eating and drinking, of speaking and singing provide the basic structures which in Christ and in the Spirit are taken up and transformed, so as to acquire eternal significance and power.

The Church itself is built up around the common meal in which all divisions are transcended, in which men and women are reconciled with one another because together reconciled with God, in which they find that they can share the good things of this earth with all their fellow human beings, because all are acknowledged as children of a common Father. The gift of speech, which in the fragmentation of human language has become divisive, a source of constant separation, in the event of Pentecost is itself healed and restored. In the gift of the Spirit from on high, the tongues of humankind, in all their diversity, are united in a common sacrifice of praise and thanksgiving. In the joy which comes from God, love and knowledge unite to open our hearts and minds to one another, to make possible a new creation in the Spirit, and thus to make of this earth the dwelling-place of a single family.

None of these things is done without the body. All have their roots in the simplest of our physical needs and actions. As Jeremy Taylor remarks about the breastfeeding of babies, 'Although other actions are more perfect and spiritual, yet this is more natural and humane; other things . . . rise higher, but this builds stronger and is like a part of the foundation, having no lustre, but much strength.' So in the mosaics of the birth and childhood of Mary, which fill the narthex of the church of St Saviour in Chora in Istanbul with colour and delight, we see the joy of parents in their children, of children in their parents as the basis of the whole future development of humankind's salvation.

Thus it is that wherever she is made known, whether at Czestochowa in Poland or at Tinos in Greece, at Chartres in France or at Zeitoun in Egypt, at Knock in Ireland or at Guadalupe in Mexico, Mary is made known as the one who gives life and courage to a whole people, and particularly to an oppressed people. She is one in whom powers and dominations are brought down and the insignificance of the humble is exalted; one who makes of this world a place of human, no less than of divine, habitation.

And this which is true in many lands, is true also in England. Here is the significance behind the simple yet mysterious command which, in the eleventh century, came to the Lady Richeldis, to build a copy of the holy house at Walsingham, so that the place might become England's Nazareth. Walsingham became in the Middle Ages one of the greatest of English places of pilgrimage. From every part of the country people came to greet Mary in this place which she had made her own. Is it surprising that among the most poignant of all sixteenth-century melodies should be one called 'Walsingham', the tune sung to the words which lament the destruction of this holy place? For centuries Walsingham, like so many other places of pilgrimage in Great Britain, lay desolate and neglected. Then in our own century, almost without people noticing it, something began to change. The holy places stirred into new life. Once again men and women came to Iona, Glastonbury, Canterbury, Walsingham and found God's healing peace and presence there.

We have remarked in previous chapters that the age in which we live is not one which finds it easy to believe in the mystery of the Word made flesh, and that is true. But it is also true that in this late and unpropitious time, God's grace, as always, is at work healing what is wounded, making up what is lacking in his creation. If for the scholars and the theologians this has been a time when they have found it difficult to speak of Mary, the people of the Church seem to have been given a new boldness to sing her praises and to rejoice in calling her blessed.

John Keble in the nineteenth century, faced with new threats to the faith which he had inherited from his father, found a new freedom and a new openness in his approach to Mary. So in our own century the unselfconscious and joyful faith of those who have flocked to Walsingham in ever increasing numbers has made its own eloquent response to the mood of despondency and faithlessness which has at times assailed the Church, and which reveals itself on both sides of many of our current controversies: in those who suggest that unless everything can be kept just as it is the Church will collapse, no less than in those who imply that unless everything can be reformed according to the latest recipe, there is no future for the Christian religion. Both attitudes reflect a fundamental lack of faith in God. Both suggest that he depends on us. The truth, as Mary teaches us, is exactly the reverse. We depend on him. It is he who rules in our affairs. It is only as we grow in that faith that the Church will be able to become, with Mary, truly 'welcoming and forgiving, praying and receiving, obedient and compassionate, confident and joyful'.

At the beginning of this century no one would have believed that Walsingham would again have become a national centre of pilgrimage, a place of ecumenical significance, attracting Roman Catholics and Orthodox, as well as Anglicans and Christians of other traditions. In the early years of Father Hope Patten's pioneering struggle to restore the shrine it would have seemed scarcely possible that within this century the shrine would again attract Archbishops of Canterbury to join in the pilgrimage. But this is what Robert Runcie did at Whitsuntide in 1980. In his sermon on that occasion he spoke of the meaning of Mary's example. 'We live in a society which trusts overmuch in words, organization, activism. Mary reminds us that quietness and longing, receptivity to the Word of God, are the beginnings of growth in the Gospel'.[5] More recently, in 1988, his successor as Archbishop, when Bishop of Bath and Wells, brought a diocesan pilgrimage to Walsingham. In his direct way, George Carey spoke of the change which had come in his own attitude towards Mary. For eighteen years he had never preached a sermon about her. 'Somehow the Protestant part of me could not find it right to speak of her place in God's order of salvation, because I was afraid of her obscuring the central place of Jesus Christ in his Church.' What changed his way of approach was a further study of the Bible itself and what it tells us of Mary's rôle in the story.

> First, I saw that she was *chosen*, and that for all time, all generations will call her blessed (Luke 1:48). Indeed the angel hails her 'O favoured one' (Luke 1:28) and later in the birth narratives Elizabeth salutes her 'Blessed are you among women' (Luke 1:42). It would be wrong then to push Mary to the circumference of the Christian story. Her place is in the centre.
>
> Second, I began to see why she was honoured in this way, I saw her humility . . . I began to see that my fear about Mary obscuring Christ was not soundly based as long as I kept to the parameters of scripture. The advice recorded in John's Gospel is always worth following 'Do whatever he tells you' (John 2:5) True Marian theology is wholly Christ-centred.
>
> Third, I saw her *availability*. She gave her consent to God's will. Fourth, I saw her as an example of God's grace . . . The best definition I know of grace is: God's Riches At Christ's Expense. The One who took up his abode in Mary was the One who sustained her, kept her and made her holy.[6]

In one of the meditations which he gave during this visit, the Archbishop spoke of the image of a well. He spoke of St Mary's Well at Nazareth, the holy well at Walsingham and the wells in the palace grounds at Wells, which give the place its name.

> The extraordinary thing about that place is its ordinariness. If you were to visit it, you would be struck by the quietness of the small pool. No great torrents of water, no spectacular waterfalls, no deafening roars of waters disgorging their immense might. On a clear day you might just be able to see the spring bubbling up at the bottom of the pond, yet from that very still place immense power emerges . . .[7]

In this image the writer sees a picture of what God longs to do in our lives.

> We think of the desert of modern life with the concentration on material possessions and its resultant poverty. We consider the dryness of the Church as it tends to be too often a shadow image of that world. Our God can still take the ordinary and make it extraordinary.[8]

The water of our daily experience can by the gift of his grace be changed into the wine of his presence.

It is remarkable that in the 1980s two successive Archbishops of Canterbury should have been drawn to Walsingham and should have seen in that place a message for the Church today. It is a message about the recovery of inner resources, stillness and quiet, receptivity and depth, qualities which may free the Church from its temptation to become simply a 'shadow image of the world', hurrying along behind the times, vainly attempting to catch up. In the light of such words spoken on such occasions, we may think that the hidden stream of thought and prayer which we have charted in these pages, and which has flowed almost unnoticed through the Anglican tradition through these last four centuries, has been more deeply influential than most have suspected. At the end of the twentieth century it seems to be bubbling up in new ways and finding a new visibility. Perhaps it is now as Anglicans begin to be drawn into unity with those from whom they have been too

long separated that there will break out a new song of praise to
her in whom the whole creation turns to God and finds in him the
unexpected, the unbelievable joy of its fulfilment.

NOTES

1   *John Paul II in Mexico: His Collected Speeches* (1979), p. 42
2   Words from the sermon by Robert Runcie, while Archbishop
     of Canterbury, at Walsingham on 26 May 1980
3   Donald Coggan, *The Prayers of the New Testament* (1974),
     p. 48
4   In *La Documentation catholique*, no. 1742, 21 May 1978,
     p. 462
5   Op. cit.
6   George Carey, *I Believe* (London 1991), p. 70
7   Ibid., p. 71
8   Ibid., p. 78

Dramatis Personae

1 **Lancelot Andrewes** (1555-1626). Successively bishop of Chichester, Ely and Winchester. Scholar, theologian, controversialist, preacher, man of prayer. One of the most important influences in the formation of the Anglican tradition.

2 **Euros Bowen** (1904-88). One of the most distinguished poets writing in Welsh in the twentieth century. Published many volumes of verse, including one bilingual volume in 1976. Also translator of Sophocles, Virgil and Athanasius and modern French poets.

3 **S.T. Coleridge** (1772-1834). Poet, critic and thinker. His influence was pervasive in the religious thought of the nineteenth century. But it is only recently that the full scope of this thought is being realized through publication of his notebooks and papers.

4 **T.S. Eliot** (1888-1965). Poet and critic; born in America, he lived and worked in England. By common consent one of the greatest writers in English of our time. Baptized into the Church in 1926, for many years churchwarden of St Stephen's, Gloucester Road, London.

5 **Richard Field** (1561-1616). Dean of Gloucester, intimate friend of Richard Hooker. His treatise *Of the Church* is one of the fullest discussions of ecclesiology from an Anglican author.

6 **Mark Frank** (1613-64). Master of Pembroke College, Cambridge. Preacher and theologian, friend of the Ferrars at Little Gidding. The article in the *Dictionary of National*

Biography describes his sermons as 'plain, sensible and evangelical discourses'.

7 **Nikolai Frederick Severin Grundtvig** (1784-1873). Dane of Danes, preacher, prophet, priest, poet, politician, scholar and educationalist. With Søren Kierkegaard, from whom he differs completely, the greatest figure of the Danish Church in his time. Decidedly not an Anglican.

8 **Reginald Heber** (1783-1826). Bishop of Calcutta from 1823 to 1826. Hymn writer and scholar of the Evangelical school. Best known for his Trinity hymn, 'Holy, holy, holy'.

9 **George Herbert** (1593-1633). Poet, son of a noble family, Public Orator in the University of Cambridge. Rejected preferment in Church or state to become vicar of the parish of Bemerton near Salisbury. Author of *The Temple* and *A Priest to the Temple*.

10 **George Hickes** (1642-1715). Literary and historical scholar. Dean of Worcester 1683-89. Non-juring Bishop of Thetford in 1694. Noted controversialist.

11 **Richard Hooker** (1554-1600). Greatest Anglican theologian since the Reformation. Master of the Temple Church in London, then Rector of Bishopsbourne near Canterbury. Wrote *The Laws of Ecclesiastical Polity;* learned, irenic, comprehensive.

12 **Fenton John Anthony Hort** (1828-92). Friend and colleague of B.F. Westcott and J.B. Lightfoot. Fellow of Trinity College, Cambridge, eminent New Testament scholar. His study, *The Way, The Truth and the Life*, is one of the outstanding works of nineteenth-century English theology.

13 **David Gwenallt Jones** (1899-1969). Welsh poet, critic and scholar. After a Marxist period he became an Anglican for a time, but eventually returned to the Methodist tradition in which he grew up.

14 **John Keble** (1792-1866). In Newman's words, 'the true and original author of the Oxford Movement'. Scholar, poet and saint. Fellow of Oriel College, Oxford, then vicar of Hursley near Winchester. One of the most attractive figures of his time.

15 **Thomas Ken** (1637-1711). Bishop of Bath and Wells, refused to take the oath of allegiance to William III in 1689. Hymn writer, preacher and saint.

16 Alexander Knox (1757-1831). Lay theologian, living in Dublin, much influenced by John Wesley in his youth. Man of wide interests, well read in the Greek Fathers, precursor of the Oxford Movement.

17 J. Saunders Lewis (1893-1985).Greatest Welsh writer of this century. One of the founders of the Welsh National party. Poet, critic, scholar and dramatist. Became a Roman Catholic in 1932.

18 Edwin Muir (1887-1959). Born in the Orkneys, lived and worked in Edinburgh, London and on the Continent. Poet and critic. Writer of a visionary quality whose true importance has not been recognized.

19 John Henry Newman (1800-91). Theologian, preacher, poet. Leader of the Oxford Movement, converted to Roman Catholicism in 1845; became a member of the Oratory. Cardinal in 1879. One of the most outstanding of English theologians; precursor of Vatican II.

20 Francis Paget (1851-1911). Bishop of Oxford in 1901, having been a senior student and Dean of Christ Church. Contributor to the collection of essays, *Lux Mundi*, 1889. Scholar and pastor in the tradition of the Oxford Movement.

21 Edward Bouverie Pusey (1800-82). Old Testament scholar, preacher and spiritual director. Professor and Canon of Christ Church, 1828-82. After Newman's conversion the unrivalled leader of the Catholic movement in the Church of England.

22 Jeremy Taylor (1613-67). Bishop of Down and Dromore in Northern Ireland. Preacher, writer and theologian. Outstanding representative of the Laudian school of Anglican theology.

23 Herbert Thorndike (1598-1672). From a Lincolnshire family, educated at Trinity College, Cambridge, fellow there in 1620. Notable Old Testament scholar and expert in patristics. In 1661, made a prebendary at Westminister Abbey, a learned systematic theologian with remarkable ecumenical insights.

24 Thomas Traherne (1638-74). Son of a Hereford shoemaker, vicar of Credenhill and chaplain to Sir Orlando Bridgman. Poet and prose writer of exceptional quality. His *Centuries of Meditations* was first published in 1908.

25 Henry Vaughan (1622-95). Welsh doctor living and practising near Brecon. Poet in the school of George Herbert; considered

by many the most deeply mystical of the Anglican poets of his century.

26 **John and Charles Wesley** (1703-91), (1707-81). Brothers, priests of the Church of England, founders of the Methodist movement, the one by his preaching and organizing ability, the other by his hymns. Two of the greatest evangelists England has ever known.

27 **Brooke Foss Westcott** (1823-1901). Bishop of Durham, New Testament scholar and theologian, Fellow of Trinity College, Cambridge. With Lightfoot and Hort, assured that the critical methods of biblical scholarship should be used for and not against the Church's faith.

28 **William Wordsworth** (1770-1850). Greatest of the English Romantic poets. In his youth strongly influenced by the French Revolution, increasingly conservative in his political and religious views as he grew older.

Index